YEAR A
LENT/ EASTER

YEAR A
LENT/ EASTER

PREACHING
THE REVISED
COMMON
LECTIONARY

Marion Soards
Thomas Dozeman
Kendall McCabe

ABINGDON PRESS
Nashville

PREACHING THE REVISED COMMON LECTIONARY
YEAR A: LENT AND EASTER

Copyright © 1992 by Abingdon Press

This book is printed on recycled, acid-free paper.

Library of Congress Cataloging-in-Publication Data

Soards, Marion L., 1952-
    Preaching the revised Common lectionary: year A / Marion L. Soards, Thomas B. Dozeman, Kendall McCabe.
    p.   cm.
    Includes indexes.
    Contents: [1] Advent, Christmas, Epiphany — [2] Lent and Easter.
    ISBN 0-687-33800-X (v. 1: alk. paper).—ISBN 0-687-33801-8 (v. 2: alk. paper)
    1. Bible—Liturgical lessons, English. 2. Bible—Homiletical use.
I. Dozeman, Thomas B. II. McCabe, Kendall, 1939—   . III. Title.
BS391.2.S59   1992
251—dc20   91-34039
                                                    CIP

Scripture quotations, unless otherwise noted, are from the New Revised Standard Version of the Bible, copyright © 1989 by the Division of Christian Education of the National Council of the Churches of Christ in the USA. Used by permission.

Scripture quotations marked RSV are from the Revised Standard Version of the Bible copyright © 1946, 1952, 1971 by the Division of Christian Education of the National Council of the Churches of Christ in the USA. Used by permission.

MANUFACTURED IN THE UNITED STATES OF AMERICA

Contents

Introduction

Now pastors and students have a systematic treatment of essential issues of the Christian year and Bible study for worship and proclamation based on the Revised Common Lectionary. Interpretation of the lectionary will separate into three parts: Calendar, Canon, and Celebration. A brief word of introduction will provide helpful guidelines for utilizing this resource in worship through the Christian year.

Calendar. Every season of the Christian year will be introduced with a theological interpretation of its meaning, and how it relates to the overall Christian year. This section will also include specific liturgical suggestions for the season.

Canon. The lectionary passages will be interpreted in terms of their setting, structure, and significance. First, the word setting is being used loosely in this commentary to include a range of different contexts in which biblical texts can be interpreted from literary setting to historical or cultic settings. Second, regardless of how the text is approached under the heading of setting, interpretation will always proceed to an analysis of the structure of the text under study. Third, under the heading of significance, central themes and motifs of the passage will be underscored to provide a theological interpretation of the text as a springboard for preaching. Thus interpretation of the lectionary passages will result in the following outline.

I. OLD TESTAMENT TEXTS

A. The Old Testament Lesson

1. *Setting*
2. *Structure*
3. *Significance*

B. Psalm

1. *Setting*
2. *Structure*
3. *Significance*

II. NEW TESTAMENT TEXTS

A. The Epistle

    1. Setting

    2. Structure

    3. Significance

B. The Gospel

    1. Setting

    2. Structure

    3. Significance

Celebration. This section will focus on specific ways of relating the lessons to liturgical acts and/or homiletical options for the day on which they occur. How the texts have been used in the Christian tradition will sometimes be illustrated to stimulate the thinking of preachers and planners of worship services.

Why We Use the Lectionary

Although many denominations have been officially or unofficially using some form of the lectionary for many years some pastors are still unclear about where it comes from, why some lectionaries differ from denomination to denomination, and why the use of a lectionary is to be preferred to a more random sampling of scripture.

Simply put, the use of a lectionary provides a more diverse scriptural diet for God's people, and it can help protect the congregation from the whims and prejudices of the pastor and other worship planners. Faithful use of the lectionary means that preachers must deal with texts they would rather ignore, but about which the congregation may have great concern and interest. The Ascension narrative, which we encounter in this volume on the Seventh Sunday of Easter, might be a case in point. Adherence to the lectionary can be an antidote to that homiletical arrogance that says, ''I know what my people need,'' and in humility acknowledges that the Word of God found in scripture may speak to more needs on Sunday morning than we even know exist, when we seek to proclaim faithfully the message we have wrestled from the text.

The lectionary may also serve as a resource for liturgical content. The psalm is intended to be a response to the Old Testament lesson, and not read as a lesson itself, but beyond that the lessons may inform the content of prayers of confession, intercession, and petition. Some lessons may be adapted as affirmations of faith, as in *The United Methodist Hymnal,* Nos. 887-889; the United Church of Christ's *Hymnal,* Nos. 429-430; and the Presbyterian *Worshipbook,* No. 30. The ''Celebration'' entries for each day will call attention to these opportunities from time to time.

Pastors and preachers in the free-church tradition should think of the lectionary as a primary resource for preaching and worship, but need to remember that the lectionary was made for them and not they for the lectionary. The lectionary may serve as the inspiration for a separate series of lessons and sermons that will include texts not in the present edition, or having chosen one of the lectionary passages as the basis for the day's sermon, the preacher may wish to make an independent choice of the other lessons to supplement and illustrate the primary text. The lectionary will be of most value when its use is not a cause for legalism but for inspiration.

Just as there are no perfect preachers, there are no perfect lectionaries. The Revised Common Lectionary, upon which this series is based, is the result of the work of many years by the Consultation on Common Texts and is a response to on-going evaluation of the *Common Lectionary* (1983) by pastors and scholars from the several participating denominations. The current interest in the lectionary can be traced back to the Second Vatican Council, which ordered lectionary revision for the Roman Catholic Church:

> The treasures of the Bible are to be opened up more lavishly, so that richer fare may be provided for the faithful at the table of God's Word. In this way a more representative portion of the holy Scriptures will be read to the people over a set cycle of years. (Walter Abbot, ed., *The Documents of Vatican II* [Piscataway, N.J.: New Century, 1974], p. 155)

The example thus set by Roman Catholics inspired Protestants to take more seriously the place of the Bible in their services and sermons, and soon many denominations had issued their own three-year cycles, based generally on the Roman Catholic model but with their own modifications. This explains why some discrepancies and variations appear in different forms of the lectionary. The Revised Common Lectionary (RCL) is an effort to increase agreement among the churches. A table at the end of the volume will list the differences between the RCL and the Roman Catholic, Episcopal, and Lutheran lectionaries. Where no entry is made, all are in agreement with the RCL.

For those unacquainted with the general pattern of the lectionary, a brief word of explanation may be helpful for sermon preparation. (1) The three years are distinguished by one of the Synoptic Gospels: Matthew in A, Mark in B, Luke in C. John is distributed over the three years with a heavy emphasis during Lent and Easter. (2) Two types of readings are used. During the periods of Advent to Epiphany and Lent to Pentecost, the readings are usually topical, that is, there is some common theme among them. During the Sundays after Epiphany and Pentecost the readings are continuous, with no necessary connection between the lessons. The preacher begins, then, with at least four preaching options: to deal with either one of the lessons on their own or to work with the dialogue between the Old Testament lesson and the gospel. Perhaps it should also be added that though the psalm is intended to be a response by the people to the Old Testament lesson—rather than as a lesson on its own—this in no way suggests that it cannot be used as the text for the sermon.

This is the second of four volumes that deal with the lessons for the entire A Cycle of the Christian year. Volume 1 dealt with Advent through the time after Epiphany. Volume 3 begins with Trinity Sunday (the First Sunday After Pentecost) and includes all the lessons for June, July, and August. Volume 4 finishes the remainder of the year, including the lessons for All Saints' Day (November 1). A new series will then be published for the B Cycle.

A note on language: We have used the term *Old Testament* in this series because that is the language employed by the Consultation on Common Texts, at least up to this point. Pastors and worship committees may wish to consider alternative terms such as *First Testament* or *Hebrew Scriptures* that do not imply that those writings somehow have less value than the rest of the Christian Bible. Another option is to refer to *First Lesson* (always from the Hebrew Scriptures), *Second Lesson* (from Acts or the epistles), and *Gospel.*

THE MIND OF CHRIST IN LENT

Lent is probably the most widely observed season in the Christian year. Churches which ignore Advent, prefer Mother's Day to Pentecost, and isolate the observance of Christmas and Easter to one day each per year are capable of mounting Lenten programs and special emphases on such a scale as to make the Easter sunrise service seem anticlimactic. The inoculation, in the form of regular church attendance for several weeks, usually works, however, for by the Sunday after Easter Day, few pietistic eruptions are to be seen remaining on the body ecclesiastical. It seems odd that so much preparation has so little payoff for Christian discipleship.

The purpose of this introduction to Lent is not to provide a different program with a guaranteed long-range payoff, but rather to help those who preach and plan worship think about what they are doing in light of that entire period of time from Ash Wednesday to the Day of Pentecost and see it as an unbroken chain of days that links us to and makes us one with the apostolic Church and its experience of the saving Christ-event.

Remember that Easter Day was originally the only day in the Christian year! The early Christians met weekly on the first day of the week to pray, break bread, and share in the apostles' reminiscences of Jesus' earthly ministry (Acts 2:42). Their meetings were characterized by an expectation of their Lord's immediate, sudden return. In this ecstatic atmosphere, one did not do long-range planning and goal setting. But even within the pages of the New Testament, we have indications that time is fast becoming a threat to Christian faith. Second Peter 3 is an effort to counter the arguments of the scoffers who deride the Christian hope. The answer that in the Lord's sight a thousand years are as one day might help relieve some of the Christian anxiety, but it did not change the fact that the Christians still had to make it through one day at a time on earthly calendars. Time, then, if it was not to be an enemy, had to be made a friend. It was through this domestication of time that the Christian year evolved.

The precise details of the evolution are impossible to know, varying as they doubtlessly did from region to region. The general outline is rather easy to discern. First, there was the weekly celebration of the Resurrection. This celebration was of the entire Paschal mystery: the Incarnation, the Crucifixion, the Resurrection and Ascension, the gift of the Spirit, and the promise of the Lord's return. There next emerged a special emphasis in the spring on the celebration of the Paschal feast in relation to the actual time of the historical event. This celebration extended itself back through the Crucifixion on Friday and the Last Supper on Thursday, thus creating the Paschal Triduum of Maundy Thursday, Good Friday, and Easter Eve, which carried over into Easter Day. We know that in Jerusalem the custom was begun of having the bishop ride a donkey into the city on the Sunday before the Passion and so inaugurate that period of observance that we call Holy Week. Just as the discrete events leading up to the Resurrection were separated for celebration, so also two other events that had been seen as part of the whole Paschal mystery were also given individual recognition: the Ascension forty days after Easter Day and the anointing by the Holy Spirit at Pentecost fifty days after.

Lent emerged in the form in which we know it as a combination of the Church's catechetical program and penitential discipline. It was catechetical in that it was the final period of intense instruction before the catechumens were brought to the bishop to be baptized at Easter. This was seen as the most appropriate time for baptism, because through that rite the catechumens fully put on Christ by dying and rising with him in the tomb of the font. One cannot overemphasize the interrelationship of baptism and instruction here. The *Apostolic Tradition* of Hippolytus (written around 250 c.e.) indicates that catechumens were to be instructed for three years and that a catechumen who was slain for the faith prior to baptism "will be justified, for he has received baptism in his blood" (chap. 19). The rule seemed to be "no baptism without catechesis." Lent may be a good time to remind ourselves of this principle, not only as we continue the traditional Lenten confirmation classes but also as we seek to establish classes for parents who will be bringing infants for baptism. As we will comment later, the readings for the Sundays of Lent in Year A are designed to be used in a nurturing process for catechumens or confirmands in preparation for Easter baptism and confirmation.

Penitential discipline came to be attached to Lent as the Church increasingly understood itself as the field where the wheat and the weeds grew together. A major disagreement in the second century had to do with how to deal with those who denied or betrayed the faith during times of persecution. Those of a more rigorous disposition were in favor of excommunication and expulsion with no second chance allowed. The more catholic view prevailed, however, so that those who had sinned were expected to perform appropriate penance and during Lent were finally prepared to be received fully back into the fellowship of the Church during Holy Week, in time to be able to celebrate the Easter mysteries once more with the faithful. It soon became customary for all Christians to use the Lenten period as a time for repentance of past sins and self-denial (hence, ''giving things up'' for Lent), even if their sins had not been of a major or notorious kind.

It is this history that is briefly described in many Ash Wednesday liturgies, such as the following from the *Handbook of the Christian Year*:

> Dear brothers and sisters in Christ: Christians have always observed with great devotion the days of our Lord's passion and resurrection. It became the custom of the church to prepare for Easter by a season of penitence, fasting, and prayer. This season of forty days provided a time in which converts to the faith were prepared for baptism into the body of Christ. It is also the time when persons who had committed serious sins and had been separated from the community of faith were reconciled by penitence and forgiveness, and restored to the fellowship of the church. The whole congregation is thus reminded of the mercy and forgiveness proclaimed in the gospel of Jesus Christ and the need we all have to renew our baptismal faith. (p. 112)

Preachers and planners of worship need, then, to keep in mind these two primary purposes of the Lenten season: the training of candidates for baptism and confirmation, and the encouragement of all the members of the congregation to renew their dedication and commitment.

Lent, then, is not a prolonged meditation upon the Passion and death of Christ, a pre-extended Good Friday. The clue to the meaning of Lent can be found by looking at the two days that frame it, Ash Wednesday and Good Friday. On Ash Wednesday, it is customary in many congregations for persons to have ashes placed upon their heads while they are being told, "Remember that you are dust, and to dust you shall return." In other words, we are confronted by the fact of our mortality in a vivid physical encounter. On Good Friday, we witness the death of another human being, and we are told that in this death we all have died. Lent certainly is intended to end at the cross, but it begins with the human condition that we all share, and it takes on the character of a pilgrimage. The First Sunday in Lent begins in the Garden of Eden as we rehearse the story of humanity's first disobedience and we learn from the epistle how death was the consequence of that action. The gospel reading for the First Sunday in Lent is about the temptation of Jesus, which occurs at the beginning of his ministry—as he begins his walk towards the cross. All of the readings for Lent provide an opportunity to examine ourselves in relation to the mystery of the cross, to examine ourselves in the light of the grace we have obtained through baptism or which we expect to obtain if we are preparing for baptism or confirmation. Because we did not celebrate Advent pretending Christmas had not happened, so we do not celebrate Lent as though we know nothing about Easter. Lent is a time of "festive fasting," in the words of Adrian Nocent:

> In the early Christian centuries the faithful thought that Christ's return would take place during the night between Holy Saturday and Easter Sunday, since that night was the center of Christian life, being the anniversary of Christ's victory and the moment when that victory became present anew. The fast that marked the Vigil, and indeed the whole Lenten fast, is festive because it is leading up to the victory and return of the Spouse. [*The Liturgical Year 2: Lent*, p. 41]

The traditional color in the West for Lent has been purple, recognizing that we are decorating for the king who is on his way to mount the throne won through the cross. The medieval English use of the "Lenten array" has been increasingly adopted by many churches.

This involves the use of unbleached linen for the paraments. Any decorative symbols such as crosses are not embroidered on, but are painted, usually in black, red, cream, or some combination of those three. The altar or communion table would be completely covered all around, giving it a coffin-like appearance. Brass or metal altarware would be replaced by a simple cross and candlesticks of wood, or the cross would be entirely draped in the same kind of unbleached material and tied at the base. The lack of any altar flowers is also appropriate during Lent in preparation for the floral explosion that usually marks the Easter proclamation.

Ash Wednesday

Old Testament Texts

The Old Testament texts explore the themes of sin and death that are central to Ash Wednesday. Joel 2:1-2, 12-17 proclaims the judgment of God on sin through the terrible Day of the Lord, while Psalm 51:1-12 is a penitentiary prayer in which the guilt of the psalmist is confessed as a basis for petitioning God for deliverance.

The Lesson: *Joel 2:1-2, 12-17*

The Terrible Day of God's Judgment

Setting. The reference to the Day of the Lord in Joel 2:1 provides important background for interpreting the Old Testament lesson. The Day of the Lord is not a definite period of time, which might occur in twenty-four hours. A better way of thinking about the Day of the Lord is to associate it with a definite divine event in time. The definite event is an action by God that determines the character of the world. The Exodus and the mission of Jesus are such events. Such actions are God's Day, and because the events reshape our world, there is always an immediacy to them.

The Day of the Lord was Israel's way of describing how God breaks into our world in special ways to bring about a new salvation. Scholars debate the particular setting in which the Day of the Lord was first used. It may have been in the context of holy war, when Israel saw that real security was not rooted in their military strength but in God. In this context, the Day of the Lord was a confession that only the wrath of God could really defeat Israel's enemies. Thus military victory was interpreted as the Day of the Lord, and its celebration required worship, because God's defeat of threatening nations embodied the essence of salvation. Over time the Day of the Lord became one of the central events in Israel's worship, and it was symbolized as bright light. Israel lived for the Day of the Lord. A close analogy in Christian tradition would be an Easter sunrise service, where the light from the rising sun also symbolizes salvation.

In order to confront the people of God with their own sins, many prophetic oracles presuppose this powerful tradition of salvation in Israel's ongoing worship. The Day of the Lord, therefore, is frequently used as a reversal—that is, as a dark and gloomy day of judgment for the people of God rather than the nations. Amos 5:18 provides an early example of this reversal. Here the prophet presents a judgment oracle by stating: "Alas for you who desire the day of the LORD! Why do you want the day of the LORD? It is darkness, not light." Joel 2:1-2, 12-17 is a prophetic oracle in the tradition of Amos, where the prophet uses a strong tradition of salvation to declare judgment on the people of God for not living out God's will. Simply put, the judgment is God's declaration of holy war on God's own people.

Structure. Joel 2:1-2 is an announcement of the judgment of God on Israel through the imagery of the great and terrible Day of the Lord. Joel 2:12-17 presents a call to repentance first from God and then from the prophet. The divine call to repentance includes Joel 2:12-13aa: "Yet even now, says the LORD, return to me with all your heart, with fasting, with weeping, and with mourning; rend your hearts and not your clothing." At the end of the divine oracle, the prophet takes center stage for the remainder of the text. Note how all pronominal references to God are now in the third person (he, v. 13) in referring to the Lord, rather than in the first person (me, v. 12). There are three stages in the prophet's speech: first, the prophet reiterates the divine call to repentance in the remainder of v. 13; second, the prophet holds out hope in v. 14 that God might repent about destroying Israel; and, third, the prophet provides cultic instructions in vv. 15-17 about how Israel might confess their sin before God.

Significance. Three important theological insights are important for preaching this text on Ash Wednesday. The first concerns divine judgment. Two conclusions follow: (1) As is frequently the case in prophetic literature, God's wrath is often far more dangerous to the people of God than to the nations. It is the people of God, after all, who know first hand the salvation of God and thus who carry a primary responsibility to follow God's will. (2) Even when the people of God experience divine wrath, judgment is not an end in itself. Rather it is a warning cry to the people of God that they are at odds with God. The importance of judgment as warning is brought to light by following the motif of the horn or trumpet. Note how the text begins in v. 1 with the prophetic call to "Blow the trumpet in Zion." In this opening verse, the trumpet is meant to call an alarm in the face of danger. Here the danger is the wrath of God. The motif does not end here, however, but returns in v. 15, where it is now meant to call the people to "sanctify" themselves in worship. Judgment is not an end in itself, but a warning cry to bring us back to God. The second theological insight is the gracious and merciful character of God of which the prophet reminds Israel in v. 13. It is because God is merciful and gracious that judgment need not be an end in itself. The third conclusion is really an extension of the previous two. God can change depending on what we do. This is illustrated in Joel 2. Even though God has declared judgment on Israel, the activity of the people of God in confessing sin can motivate change in God. As the prophet states in v. 13, God is able to "repent of evil."

The Response: *Psalm 51:1-17*

Coming to Grips with Guilt

Setting. Psalm 51 is either a prayer song or a petitionary prayer. The psalm presents a powerful and sustained confession of guilt that evolves into a plea for divine deliverance. The historical commentary at the beginning of the psalm invites the reader to interpret the petition as coming from David after the prophet Nathan has unmasked his guilt of sleeping with Bathsheba and in killing her husband, Uriah, the Hittite. The historical setting underscores that the psalm is meant to be a liturgical guide of how we approach God at those times when we feel the most alienated.

Structure. Psalm 51:1-17 focuses on the psalmist's confrontation of guilt and the plea for grace because of God's character. Psalm 51:1-17 separates into four parts. Verses 1-2 are a petition for mercy; vv. 3-5 are an acknowledgment of guilt; vv. 6-12 are a plea for deliverance, and vv. 13-17 are a vow of praise. Examination of this structure will clarify the significance of the psalm for worship on Ash Wednesday.

Significance. Psalm 51 reinforces the conclusions from Joel 2. First, the fact that the psalmist is approaching God in confession underscores the central point in Joel 2 that divine judgment is not an end in itself, because mercy constitutes the character of God at the most fundamental level. This insight provides the basis for the petition in v. 1. In fact, Psalm 51 might function as the liturgy for the worship service to which the prophet called the people in Joel 2:15: "Blow the trumpet in Zion; sanctify a fast; call a solemn assembly." Second, as in Joel 2, judgment is not necessarily the final word, because God is merciful and gracious. Thus just as the prophet called Israel to repentance in Joel 2:13 by reminding them of God's merciful character, so also the psalmist begins the petition by reciting the same confessional formula: "Have mercy on me, O God, according to your steadfast love; according to your abundant mercy." And, third, both the prophetic call to repentance in Joel 2 and the petitionary prayer in Psalm 51 are rooted in the conviction that God can change—that a divine decision to judge can be reversed.

Yet at this point Psalm 51 also departs from Joel 2 in at least one significant way. The more distant prophetic perspective in Joel 2:18 of a new salvation underscored both how God is able to change and how that change is motivated by the actions of the people of God. Psalm 51:1-17 never achieves the distant perspective of Joel 2 because it is embedded in the moment of confession itself. Thus Psalm 51 does not enter into a discussion about the gracious character of God, and it does not contemplate how human actions might motivate divine change. Instead, it confronts the "truth" (v. 6) of God directly, which provides the backdrop for two stark realities: one, we are born in sin and thus the equivalent of nuclear fallout in the presence of God (vv. 3-5); and, two, only God can decontaminate us (vv. 6-12). Ash Wednesday is meant to confront us with the same "truth."

New Testament Texts

The regard of the world and the regard of God for faithful servants of God is quite different, so that a Christian must decide for whom and to what end one is at work. The passages from Matthew give directions for practicing one's piety—both warning against using piety to make an impression on humans and admonishing the practice of true devotion. Paul's words to the Corinthians inform them that those doing God's will live faultlessly before others, but they do not necessarily make a smooth impression on people.

The Epistle: *II Corinthians 5:20b–6:10*

Working Together with God

Setting. In his second letter to the Corinthians, Paul writes at length about the character of his ministry, which was apparently being criticized by some in the Church (see II Corinthians 2:14–6:13). From 2:14 through 5:19 Paul discusses Christian ministry; then, in 5:20-21 he draws a conclusion to his reflections, which also functions as a bridge to the full blown appeal that follows in 6:1–7:4 (perhaps omitting 6:14–7:1—see a scholarly commentary on the problems associated with this passage).

Structure. Translators and commentators handle the material in these verses differently. Some recognize the "break" between chapters 5 and 6, understanding 5:20-21 to be part of a larger statement in 5:11-21. Others see a relationship between 5:20-21 and the foregoing passage(s), but they understand that Paul's word *therefore* strikes a new direction in the letter, so that 5:20-21 is better held in relationship with 6:1-10. Increasingly, the latter assessment is the norm among interpreters, and the lectionary (modified from previous editions) falls in line with current thinking. The section, 5:20–6:2, is a striking summary statement of the nature of Paul's ministry, which makes an appeal to the Corinthians; and 6:3-10 elaborates the point by illustrating the character of Paul's ministry as it is seen from two different points of view: the human and the divine.

Significance. Although Paul seems actually to be writing alone, he does not cast himself as an individual operating independently; rather, he views himself in the context of his fellow Christian missionary associates (Timothy, Titus, and others), as is clear in his steady use of "we" instead of "I." In 5:18-19 Paul made twin statements: (1a) all things are from God (1b) who has reconciled us to himself through Christ (1c) and has given to us the ministry of reconciliation; (2a) God (2b) in Christ was reconciling the world to himself (2c) and establishing among us the word of reconciliation. Then, in 5:20–6:2 Paul builds on the third element (item "c") of the double statements. Paul declares what his ministry is about and gives details about his doing of the ministry of reconciliation. Paul does not speak abstractly, but with the current situation in view; so that, finally, he takes Isaiah 49:8 as a text to argue (in "precedent-in-prophecy," not "proof-from-prophecy," style) that "now" is the promised eschatological "time of favor" and the "day of salvation." Paul's reading of current reality is from the eschatological perspective of God's ultimate triumph in salvation.

Paul understands that God works in and through Jesus Christ to transform the lives of believers into harmony with God's own purposes; thus Paul can say that "for our sake he made him to be sin who knew no sin, so that in him we might become the righteousness of God." For Paul, the phrase *the righteousness of God* is a coded expresssion, naming God's saving work. Here the apostle means that inherent in God's gift of salvation in Christ is the demand for a life of faithful service on the part of those who experience salvation—strikingly this obedient service comes as part of the gift of salvation.

Verses 3-10 support Paul's appeal to the Corinthians to "be

reconciled'' by relating something of the apostle's own methods in ministry. In 6:3-4*a* Paul declares his ''blameless'' style of service. The cryptic remark in v. 4*a*, ''but as servants of God we have commended ourselves in every way,'' means simply that Paul consistently does what God would have him do—in obedience. Then, 6:4*b*-10 enumerates or describes, in grand rhetorical form, the contour and content of the apostle's ministry. Despite many translations, v. 6 should read ''the Holy Spirit,'' not ''holiness of spirit.'' This is evident from the mention of the synonymous ''power of God'' in v. 7. Throughout these verses—and throughout the entirety of 2:14–7:4— Paul presents an ironic theological truth: God's point of view and a purely human point of view are different from each other. Indeed that which appears to be ''nothing'' in the eyes of the present age, if done in faithful service to God's will, is ''everything''—because of God's righteousness.

The Gospel: *Matthew 6:1-6, 16-21*

The Nature of True Piety

Setting. We encounter another portion of the Sermon on the Mount. Following the Beatitudes, Matthew collects a series of Jesus' teachings on a range of topics. We examined the sections on ''salt and light,'' the Law, anger, and piety and human relations during the weeks between the celebration of the Baptism of the Lord and the Transfiguration. Following those portions of the Sermon come teachings about adultery, divorce, oaths, retaliation, and love for enemies. The initial section of our texts for this week follows that material. The lectionary omits 6:7-15, the Lord's Prayer with its didactic introduction and conclusion. As is the case throughout the Sermon, all of the occurrences of *you* are plural forms, so that this is teaching for the community, not merely for the individual.

Structure. These verses are like five pearls on a string, though it is helpful to view v. 1 as an introductory thematic statement; vv. 2-6, 16-18 as a series of examples of the theme with concluding words of

assurance; and vv. 19-21 as a metaphorical conclusion to the theme
with an explanation of the logic behind the teaching. Thus,

Theme: Practice your piety before God, not people (v. 1)
Examples: Alms-giving (vv. 2-4a) + assurance (v. 4b)
            Prayer (vv. 5-6a) + assurance (v. 6b)
            Fasting (vv. 16-18a) + assurance (v. 18b)
Conclusion: Laying up treasure (vv. 19-20) + logic (v. 21).

Significance. At the outset of sermon preparation, one must make a
crucial decision: Is this or is this not an occasion for a didactic sermon?
The ideas expressed in v. 1 and vv. 19-21 may be clear and readily
accessible to members of modern congregations, but our experience
suggests that very few contemporary church-goers will really
understand the first-century Jewish customs referred to in the
examples of alms-giving, prayer, and fasting. Certainly there is a time
and a place for a teaching-style of preaching, but should instruction
occur on Ash Wednesday? Probably not.

A more productive line for dealing with this text or these texts in the
context of Ash Wednesday may be to work with one or more of three
crucial issues raised explicitly or implicitly by this passage when it is
read in its liturgical context. First, these verses are wrestling with the
subject of our ultimate concerns. What really matters to us as humans,
as people who profess Christian faith? (And, on Ash Wednesday we
can assume we are working with a group of professing believers.) As
we come before God on Ash Wednesday, why have we come? And as
we leave worship, what difference does our having been here make?
As we depart from confessing our sins and taking on the ashes as a sign
of our genuine contrition, about what do we care as we return to our
everyday lives? Is it God, or have we merely attempted to get God off
our backs by repenting so that we can get back to doing what we are
really about? Jesus' words are more than practical advice about piety,
they are a strong directive to give God first-place in our lives, so that
God's concerns become ours. This line of thought elaborates and
helps us understand the difficult words of Jesus that immediately
precede the Ash Wednesday text, "Be perfect therefore, as your
heavenly Father is perfect" (Matthew 5:48).

Second, the words of assurance, issued as a refrain in the teachings on alms, prayer, and fasting, speak of our God who sees and who is in secret. The image of God is highly eschatological, for it relates to a full form of judgment that will reward, and thus make known, even what was previously unknown. Nothing is beyond God, not even secrecy. God knows our true motives. We come on an Ash Wednesday—as on all the days of our lives—before such a God. The stark reality that confronts us challenges our piety, threatening to undo false motives but promising that true godliness will be rewarded even if it goes completely unnoticed by others. The image of God is simultaneously awe-inspiring and deeply comforting.

Third, hearing these verses in the context of Ash Wednesday worship, wherein one normally receives the imposition of the ashes, should produce a high degree of cognitive dissonance. What does it mean to listen to Jesus' directives to the modesty of true devotion and, then, to go forth with the sign of the cross plastered on our foreheads? Are we in danger of parading our piety? Do we defy our Lord in order to demonstrate our faith? Why do we wear these ashes? Again, we are driven to examine our inner motives and to ask whether God's causes are ours. The real tension between the words of scripture and the patterns of our practice can be a creative tension, which rubs us just raw enough to allow the oil beneath the ashes to become a healing oil that is bonding the ashes of repentance to our bodies while the sign of the cross of Christ becomes the true character of our very selves.

Ash Wednesday: The Celebration

Thoughtful planning for today involves the need to balance the individual and corporate nature of the event. Joel calls for a gathering of the people, Paul discusses what it should mean for a community to be in ministry, and Jesus speaks in the plural *you* about the duties of prayer, fasting, and almsgiving. Attention to the communal concerns is important if the intensely personal experience of the imposition of ashes is observed. Catechumens and penitents alike need to be helped to see themselves as a community on pilgrimage through Lent to Easter, and therefore they need to have and practice a concern for one another. How can prayer, fasting, and almsgiving be given a corporate rather than merely an individual expression?

Psalm 51, as it appears in the lectionary, is intended as a response to the Joel lesson. In some Ash Wednesday liturgies, it also appears as part of the imposition rite. To avoid duplication, Psalm 103:6-18 might be used as an alternative (preferably after Joel). The Revised Common Lectionary lists Isaiah 58:1-12 as an alternative Old Testament lesson, though it was recently used on the Fourth Sunday After Epiphany. If it is not used, vv. 6-9*b* in unison or responsively may serve as a response to the epistle and a preparation for hearing the gospel text. If it is used, then selected verses of Joel can serve as a call to worship.

The hymn "Lord, Who Throughout These Forty Days" is being introduced in many hymnals for the first time, but frequently it is set to tunes unfamiliar to those very congregations where acceptance of liturgical change is greatly desired. The tune Maitland, known to many congregations as "Must Jesus Bear the Cross Alone," fits the text well. The unconscious association with the older hymn will help reinforce the message of the more recent one.

The ancient custom of burning the palms of the previous Passion/Palm Sunday to obtain this year's ashes is practiced by many churches. The burning is not done in church or as a separate service, however. It provides a practical answer to the question of what to do with the palms that have had a religious character imposed on them. It also communicates on a deeper level a truth about the transient nature of earthly joy. Some pastors produce the ashes by burning slips of paper on which the congregation has made some sign or mark in token of individual sins. This practice may reinforce the subjective element too markedly because it identifies our sinfulness with individual actions rather than as a condition of our existence.

Where imposition of ashes is being introduced and people are clearly wrestling with the tension between inward piety and outward witness (see the commentary on the gospel text above), a brief rite of cleansing might be employed at the end of the service in which the ashes are removed by a cloth dampened in water and perfumed oil. Some formula such as "Your sins have been cast into the depths of the sea" might be employed. Or simply, "Cleansed and forgiven, go in peace to love and serve the Lord."

First Sunday in Lent

Old Testament Texts

The themes of sin and death that were central to Ash Wednesday are carried over into the First Sunday in Lent. These themes, however, are explored somewhat differently. Rather than a prophetic announcement of divine judgment against the people of God in the form of the Day of the Lord, as was the case in Joel 2, Genesis 2:15-17; 3:1-7 explores the consequences of sin for all humans and for the creation itself through the stark imagery of exposed nakedness in a garden that is quickly vanishing. Psalm 32 provides liturgical language of hope by showing us how to petition for God's grace, even when we are all too aware of our weakness and shame.

The Lesson: *Genesis 2:15-17; 3:1-7*

Shame as Death

Setting. Our interpretation of the Old Testament lesson will expand the boundaries of Genesis 3:1-7 to include Genesis 2:25 as an introduction to this section in order to explore the meaning of shame that runs throughout this text. Shame occurs in Genesis 2:25 in conjunction with nakedness, and it is implied again in Genesis 3:7 when the motif of nakedness reappears. The concept of shame is important in this Lenten season, for, as we will see, it underscores how sin has consequences that go far beyond particular human actions. But to understand the biblical use of shame, we must distance ourselves from its every day use in contemporary culture. We often think of shame as immoral action. For example, a particular kind of conduct such as stealing may be described as being shameful. Hence the person who has stolen something ought to feel ashamed. Although this is part of the meaning of shame in the Old Testament, it is not its primary meaning.

Shame is not first and foremost about our sinful actions or even about our subjective feelings concerning wrongful actions. Rather, shame describes an objective situation or a state-of-being where things are out of sync, because the opposite of what was intended in fact happens. The story of the battle between David and his son Absalom in II Samuel 19 provides an illustration. In this story David is being defeated by Absalom, who desires his father's throne and is in the process of taking it with a superior army. When defeat looks inevitable, David's remaining loyal troops go out to fight to the death for their king and, surprisingly, they defeat Absalom in spite of the odds. So far so good. Yet upon returning victoriously to the city, they find David mourning his lost son rather than praising their victory. Although David's actions are inappropriate (and indeed shameful, see v. 5), nevertheless, it is his troops who are in a situation of shame, because the opposite of what they had intended by defending David with their lives in fact happens—David is weeping. Consequently, we read in v. 3 that "the people stole into the city that day as people steal in who are ashamed when they flee in battle." Even though David has acted shamefully, shame itself is bigger than his action and actually becomes a distorted state of affairs for his troops, which they too must now endure.

Genesis 2–3 is also about shame as both wrongful action and a distorted state of affairs. An outline of the structure of the lectionary lesson will provide the framework for us to see how the sin of eating the forbidden fruit introduces shame into the very fabric of creation and how this shame is itself death, which must now be endured by all humanity.

Structure. Genesis 2:15-17, 25–3:7 can be divided between an initial account of humanity living innocently in the garden (Genesis 2:15-17, 25) and the introduction of sin with its consequence of shame (Genesis 3:1-7). Each section separates into three parts, so that the changing response of the man and the woman to nakedness provides the unifying link throughout the text. The text could be outlined in the following manner:

I. The Shame-Free World of the Garden
   A. Humanity in the garden (2:15)
   B. The command not to eat of the tree of the knowledge of good and evil with its consequence of death (2:16-17)
   C. The innocence of humanity: naked and no shame (2:25)
II. The Introduction of Shame with the Fall of Humanity
   A. The serpent in the garden (3:1)
   B. The enticement to eat of the tree of the knowledge of good and evil with the promise of special knowledge rather than death (3:2-5)
   C. The loss of innocence: naked and ashamed (3:6-7)

Significance. We all know Genesis 2–3 as the biblical account of "the Fall." Most would agree that the central event of the Fall is the eating of forbidden fruit. With this disobedient action, humanity trespassed beyond the inherent boundaries of creation, and in so doing they fulfill the serpent's enticement that they will know good and evil, because, even though they were created for good, their action now embodies evil. Although this interpretation is correct, the story is about much more than the disobedient action of humanity: It is about the consequences of their action for all of humanity and for creation itself.

The motif of nakedness that concludes each section (2:25, 3:7), and, especially the changing response of the man and woman to it, underscores how the Fall is a story about shame—that is, how wrongful action brings about a permanently distorted state of affairs, which must now be endured by all, regardless of motive or subsequent action. Note how the utopian state of the garden is summed up in Genesis 2:25 with the blunt statement about nakedness without shame. This is certainly a statement about the innocence of humanity, but it is also more. By specifically using the motif of shame, the writer is also saying something about creation itself. Creation is structured in the way that God has intended it to be as an idyllic garden. Thus, nakedness is not just the innocence of humanity, it also signifies the proper state of affairs in creation. The return of the motif of nakedness in Genesis 3:7 as something of which the man and woman have now become self-conscious and thus wish to eliminate underscores their loss of innocence in the light of their disobedient action: they now know good and evil. But this action has further consequences, for once the inherent boundaries of creation are trespassed, the utopian world of the garden itself becomes permanently shattered. The shattering of the garden is a distorted state of affairs that introduces shame into the very fabric of creation, which must now be endured by all. The situation of shame and the alienation of knowing that no action of our own can reverse the situation is the death of which the humans were warned in Genesis 2:17. The knowledge of good and evil carries an enormous price tag.

The Response: *Psalm 32*

Distress, Guilt, and Deliverance

Setting. Psalm 32 has been characterized as either a prayer song or as an individual song of thanksgiving. What is clear regardless of the exact form-critical description is that the psalm presupposes that the singer has already experienced the salvation of God in being rescued from a threatening situation. Because of this the psalm includes both language of confession and challenge to other worshipers. The language of confession comes through in vv. 6-7 and the language of challenge is evident in the wisdom admonitions of vv. 1-2, 8-11.

Structure. A clear structure of Psalm 32 is difficult to determine. Several transitions are evident: Wisdom language begins the psalm in vv. 1-2. Verses 3-7 include a description of distress, guilt, and deliverance, and vv. 8-9 could be words from the psalmist addressed to other worshipers, or they could be addressed to the psalmist in which case they are spoken either by God or a priest(?).

Significance. The language of Psalm 32 complements the emphasis on sin as shame in Genesis 2–3. To be noted in particular are the terms for sin in the opening verses. Here the words for human evil include specific actions of rebellion by humans (v. 1, transgression and sin) and the distortion that results from them (v. 2, iniquity). Salvation and, more specifically, human fulfillment require that God not only forgive our wrongful actions but also address the distorted state of affairs that follow. The psalmist makes it clear that the human action which prompts divine forgiveness is acknowledgment of sin and confession (v. 5).

New Testament Texts

These seemingly different texts have in common the use of a typological approach to reading scripture and commenting on Jesus' significance. In Matthew the typology is implicit, Jesus relives the story of Moses and Israel in the wilderness; whereas, in Romans, the typological approach is explicit: Adam is interpreted as an antitype for Jesus; Adam personifies the sin-flawed old creation, and Jesus embodies the perfect new creation.

The Epistle: *Romans 5:12-19*

God's Old and New Creation

Setting. Paul's letter to the church at Rome is a rich complex of the apostle's theological reflections on a wide range of crucial topics. The body of the letter is quite extensive, running at least from 1:11 through 11:36 (some argue for 15:13 as the end of the "body" of the letter). Paul sounded the theme of this epistle in 1:16-17, and then he ruminates in relation to some of his own concerns and the interests of the Roman Christians throughout the rest of the letter. This passage is part of a section comprising chapters 5–8 wherein Paul contemplates the life of Christian freedom created by God in Jesus Christ. The Roman Christians who seem to have questions about the value of law observance would find these remarks about freedom especially important.

Structure. The complete discussion of Adam and Christ runs from 5:12-21. The passage falls into three parts: vv. 12-14 refer to sin and its consequences, especially death; vv. 15-17 consider the gift of grace and its effects, especially life; and vv. 18-21 juxtapose and repeatedly reiterate the contrast between Adam's sin and humanity's condemnation and Christ's righteousness and humanity's acquittal. Verses 20-21 elaborate and extrapolate from the previous verses (18-19), so that one can omit or include these in the reading without altering the sense of the text in a significant way.

Significance. Modern readers and hearers of this text will have at least two problems with this passage. First, they will find the typological argument strange. Second, the extreme individualism of the modern world—especially in Europe and, even more, in North America—is out of sync with the corporate mentality behind this passage. Even thinking in the most symbolic fashion will not overcome our resistance to the idea that what one person does—be it Adam or Christ—can have a "spiritual" effect on the whole human race. We do not, and perhaps cannot, think in these terms. Thus the use of this profound passage for preaching and worship carries with it real difficulties.

There are two possible routes for handling this problem. One can either engage in didactic activity—and unlike Ash Wednesday this may be a good time for such proclamation—or one can shift the metaphor to preserve the sense of Paul's discussion without taking on the hazards of his style of argument. If one chooses the path of the teaching sermon, there are many helpful commentaries that should be carefully studied (for example, the commentaries of P. J. Achtemeier, C. K. Barrett, K. Barth, C. E. B. Cranfield, J. D. G. Dunn, E. Käsemann, M. Luther, and P. W. Meyer—to name a few important contributions). In the following remarks, the second path is taken.

This text is about creation—the old sin-dominated world and the new grace-filled order. The ways of the old creation—sin, disobedience, and death—are set against the realities of the new creation—righteousness, obedience, and life. The old order (typified by Adam) was driven by the power of sin, or opposition and isolation from God, but the new order (manifested in Christ) operates by the power of grace, or compliance and connection with God's will.

Paul takes for granted the existence of evil or sin. Like other first-century Jews, he shows no interest in accounting for the origin of evil, even in saying that Adam sinned. The theodicy issue is not resolved. Paul's concern is to decry the dastardly nature of sin with its deplorable consequence: death. Against the horrible reality of sin and death, Paul declares the extravagant goodness of God's grace, which overturns and undoes the power of sin and imbues the new order with life. Paul does not account for the origin of evil, but he proclaims the origin of grace—it is a free gift from God. It may take a little effort and illustration to persuade most people that there is real evil in the world, but perhaps the case is worth making. Increasing numbers of mainstream Christians sound like adherents of Christian Science when they say that evil may only appear to be evil because of our limited human perspective. This "new age" thinking is out of line with biblical perspectives that take evil with absolute seriousness. Only when we take sin seriously can we fully appreciate the wonderful character of grace. Our lives are transformed and renewed as part of God's redemptive love through Jesus Christ. This is the gospel message, and the major emphasis of Paul's text is the great goodness of God's grace.

The Gospel: *Matthew 4:1-11*

The Temptation of the Son of God

Setting. During the season after the Epiphany we encountered Matthew 3:13-17 as we reflected upon the Baptism of the Lord. We saw how Jesus, the Son of God, fulfilled "all righteousness" and all of Israel's prophetic expectations in quite unexpected ways. The text for this Sunday follows in the wake of the story of Jesus' baptism and advances the themes of Jesus' Sonship and his realization of Israel's hopes. Both the baptism and the temptation are major moments of preparation for Jesus as he approaches his public ministry, which begins formally in the next story starting at 4:12.

Structure. Matthew's story of the three temptations of Jesus is far more elaborate than the comparable material in Mark 1:12-13, but it is very much like the story in Luke 4:1-13. Interpreters most often understand that Matthew took the beginning (4:1) and the ending (4:11*b*) of this story from Mark, and that the material in 4:2-11*a*, which parallels the Lukan account, comes from Q or some other source available to Matthew and Luke. Independent of all source theories, the basic incident is told in 4:1-2*a*, 11*b*: "Then Jesus was led up by the Spirit into the wilderness to be tempted by the devil. He fasted forty days and forty nights. . . . Then the devil left him, and suddenly angels came and waited on him.'' The detailed account of the exchanges between the tempter and Jesus in 4:2*b*-11*a* develops definite theological concerns.

Significance. We learned of Jesus' divine Sonship in the accounts of his conception, birth, and early childhood; and in the story of his baptism, the heavenly voice declared his identity. At his baptism, Sonship and obedience were brought together explicitly in Jesus' stated commitment to fulfill all righteousness. Here, in an even more explicit way, we see Jesus defining the nature of his Sonship and, in turn, the nature of his ministry. Matthew gives details in telling this story that heighten the connection between Jesus and Israel's past. We recall Moses' experience at Sinai when we read that Jesus fasted "forty days and forty nights"—the time of Moses' stay, without food or drink, on Sinai (Exod. 34:28). Moreover, the Son of God Jesus relives the desert experiences of Israel, but he does not give in to temptation, so that he actually fulfills or redeems Israel's history.

The temptations are the testing of the truth and meaning of Jesus' Sonship. The devil challenges, "If you are the Son of God," thus making plain the character of the controversy. The tempter's words cleverly cut two ways: They question the veracity of Jesus' identity as Son, and they attempt to provoke him to prove his identity by becoming a miracle-worker, which was the standard posture of ancient, so-called "divine men." Jesus refuses to fall prey to the devil's ploy, responding with a quotation of scripture to say that the true evidence of his Sonship is not the demonstration of his power, but the faithful trust he manifests in relation to God's will. The devil quickly picks up on Jesus' line by inviting him to demonstrate radical trust in God by throwing himself off the pinnacle of the Temple. Satan calls for reckless self-abandonment in a fantastic fling of sensational leaping, and he joins Jesus in quoting scripture to illustrate or document his point. (Even Satan can quote the Bible!) Yet, Jesus once again refuses to take the devil's bait. Jesus sees Satan's scheme for what it is; he is tempting Jesus to tempt God. Jesus' reply shows that he waits on God, he does not provoke God. In turn, the devil makes a third plea. He offers Jesus power, position, and privilege—all at only one price! Jesus must turn from the God who calls him to fulfill all righteousness and turn to Satan who offers him so much for seemingly so little. The truth of Jesus' Sonship shines through as he authoritatively replies to Satan. The magisterial dismissal, "Begone, Satan!" introduces still another quotation of scripture. Jesus refuses to allow Satan to wrestle scripture from his hands; rather, he shows himself to be the rightful interpreter of the sacred text—a role he will play throughout Matthew's account.

The temptations invite Jesus to abuse his Sonship, to use God rather than to be used by God—to refuse God in order to have things for himself. But Jesus shows his true Sonship and power by defeating the tempter through simply remaining loyal to God. Once again Matthew tells us that Sonship means faithful obedience, and in Jesus Christ we see the one who knew and did God's will.

Lent 1: The Celebration

Today's lessons contrast the temptation of Adam with the temptation of Christ. Paul explains that in Adam's temptation and fall we see our own sinfulness manifested, and in Christ's victory over temptation we see the victory that God makes possible for us and that we are preparing to celebrate at Easter. The Middle Ages made much of this contrast between Adam and Christ in its devotional works and liturgical art. It expanded the analogy to include Eve, who disobeyed God's word, and Mary, who was obedient, and even to include the tree in the Garden, which brought death, and the "tree" of Calvary, which brings eternal life. A frequent image portrays Christ hanging on the cross while his blood flows down upon Adam's skull at its base. Such a woodcut might serve as the cover for today's bulletin.

In one of his sermons, St. Augustine makes clear the redemptive relationship that exists between Christ and us in terms of today's theme of temptation:

> Christ transformed us in himself when he allowed himself to be tempted by Satan. Just now in the Gospel we heard that the Lord Jesus Christ was tempted in the wilderness by the devil. . . . Why was he tempted? Because in him you were being tempted. Christ took his flesh from you and in return gave you the salvation that resides in him; he took your death for himself and gave you his life; he took the shame you deserved and gave you the honor that was his. Consequently, he took

your temptation and gave you his victory. If we are tempted in him, we also overcome the devil in him. [Quoted in Nocent, *The Liturgical Year 2: Lent,* pp. 71-72]

Augustine's comment serves to remind us that today's hymns should emphasize our dependence on Christ in the struggle against sin. Some of the Church's "fight songs" that are particularly popular during Lent can easily give the impression that we are slugging it out by ourselves with Christ cheering us on from the grandstand in the sky. The tone of today's lessons calls for such hymns as "Forty Days and Forty Nights," "Lord, Who Throughout These Forty Days," "Jesus, Lover of My Soul," "O Love, How Deep, How Broad, How High," and "In the Hour of Trial." "Am I a Soldier of the Cross" needs to wait for a more martial text.

Second Sunday in Lent

Old Testament Texts

The themes of sin and death, which have been central to the Lenten Old Testament lessons up to this point, give way to divine promise of life and blessing in Genesis 12:1-4a. Psalm 122 takes the divine promise of life and blessing into the setting of worship, where it functions both as a song of praise to God for the gift of peace and salvation, and as encouragement to the worshiper to seek the security of God's grace.

The Lesson: *Genesis 12:1-4*a

The Working Out of God's Blessing

Setting. Genesis 12:1-4a is a transitional text in the book of Genesis. It provides a hinge between the universal history in Genesis 1–11 and the more focused history of the Israelite ancestors in the remainder of the book. A brief overview of the thematic movement in Genesis 1–11 will provide important background for interpreting the central motifs in Genesis 12:1-4a.

In many ways Genesis 1–11 is an extended story about the victory of sin and death over life, for it narrates how the harmonious world of Genesis 1–2 is thrown out of balance through a series of "falls." We examined the initial "Fall" last week in Genesis 3, in the story where humans trespass beyond the inherent boundaries of creation by eating the forbidden fruit in Genesis 3. This action has permanent consequences for creation. The most immediate consequence is that the "ground" is cursed (Hebrew, *'ārûr*) along with the serpent in Genesis 3:4, 17. With the divine curse firmly in place, the world blemishes quickly almost like an ink stain that rapidly moves through the fibers of a cotton shirt. The divine curse moves from the ground to persons when Cain murders Abel in Genesis 4. Even God tries to wash it out with the flood in Genesis 6–9 but this, too, is a failure. The flood waters barely recede before the curse resurfaces by being passed from person to person when Noah curses Canaan in Genesis 9:25. The persistent and growing power of the cursed creation is the stage upon which we must place Genesis 12:1-4*a*. The content of these verses signals a new act in the drama.

Structure. Genesis 12:1-4*a* separates into four parts: the divine command for Abraham to leave his present life situation for a new land in v. 1, a series of divine promises that defines God's relationship to Abraham in v. 2, the effect of God's new relationship with Abraham on the nations in v. 3, and a concluding note about Abraham's obedience in v. 4*a*.

Significance. In contrast to the growing power of the cursed creation in Genesis 1–11 that was outlined above, the central motif of Genesis 12:1-4*a* is blessing (Hebrew, *bārak*). It occurs no less than five times in three verses: God will bless Abraham, Abraham's name will be a blessing, God will bless those who bless Abraham, and finally all the families of the earth will be blessed by Abraham. An interpretation of this motif both in the larger context of Genesis 1–11 and within the structure of Genesis 12:1-4*a* will provide insight into the nature of God's grace and how that grace provides mission for the people of God.

First the motif of blessing in the larger context of Genesis 1–11: The blessing of God was rooted in the original creation, where it was bestowed both on humans as a mandate for them to be fruitful and to multiply in Genesis 1:22, 28 and on the Sabbath in Genesis 2:3. Although the motif reappears in Genesis 5:2 and 9:1—both are repetitions of the creation blessing that urged humans to be fruitful and to multiply—it is subordinated to the growing power of the cursed creation and, indeed, appears to vanish completely with Sarah's barrenness in Genesis 11:30. Yet, just when the power of the cursed creation appears to have reached its full extent in the loss of all fruitfulness in Sarah (Genesis 11:10-32), God reintroduces the motif as promise to Abraham in Genesis 12:1-4*a*. This speech is more about

God than Abraham. Six times God makes an "I" statement to
Abraham. The cumulative effect of the divine "I" statements is that
even though Abraham is commanded to act in the opening verse, he
seems strangely passive in the light of God's overwhelming promise
of blessing. The divine blessing signifies God's commitment to
combat the power of sin and death, for it is the antidote to the cursed
creation.

Second, an interpretation of the structure of Genesis 12:1-4a will
demonstrate how the blessing of God on Abraham provides mission
for the people of God. The divine speech to Abraham separates into
three parts: it moves from command (v. 1), to God's relationship with
Abraham (v. 2), to Abraham's relationship to the nations (v. 3). The
structure illustrates how Genesis 12:1-4a is a "small" story taking
place on a one person stage in contrast to the grand drama of Genesis
1–11, where all of creation provided the setting for larger-than-life
conflict. In the smaller drama of Genesis 12:1-4a, God approaches
only Abraham directly, leaving the nations with indirect access to
God's blessing through Abraham, and this gives rise to mission. The
mission of Abraham and, indeed, of all the people of God through the
ages is to pass along the antidote to the cursed creation and to continue
the journey to a new land. In preaching this text, you may wish to
reflect on concrete ways that your congregation has received divine
blessing, how they might pass this blessing along to your larger
community, and what risks this may pose for them.

The Response: *Psalm 121*

Risks and Blessings

Setting. The central clue to determining the setting of Psalm 121 is
the question that is posed in v. 1. Several problems concerning both
genre and structure arise when one attempts to interrelate this question
with the larger psalm. Some scholars suggest that the psalm is a
dialogue between a worshiper and a priest, with the worshiper posing
the question in v. 1, which the priest then answers in v. 2. The

dialogue continues with the worshiper speaking in v. 3 and the priest in v. 4 and in vv. 5-8. The problem with this interpretation of the psalm is that the first person suffixes in v. 2 ("my help") doesn't fit well as an answer to the layperson. Thus another structure will be suggested in the present interpretation. The question and answer format does suggest, however, that the hymn is some form of dialogue that takes place in the context of worship. Some scholars suggest that it was an entrance liturgy used when pilgrims entered the Temple.

Structure. The question and answer (or perhaps better, confessional) format is clear and must be maintained in structuring the psalm. Thus the question in v. 1 stands apart. The remainder of the psalm can be interpreted as the answer to the question. The answer begins with confession in v. 2 (note the first person) and then moves to an oracle of salvation (note the third person "he" throughout vv. 3-8).

Significance. The psalm provides commentary on Genesis 12:1-4*a* in two ways. First, the question and answer format provides a liturgical response to the promise of blessing in Genesis 12:1-4*a* which takes seriously the risks involved in following God. Second, the salvation oracle in vv. 3-8 restates the content of blessing in a worship setting. The question and answer format of Psalm 121 lends itself well for use during the worship service either at the beginning of the service as an entrance liturgy or at the close of a service as a congregational response and word of assurance of the promise of blessing that is central to the Old Testament lesson.

New Testament Texts

The epistle reading from Romans forms a parallel to the lesson from Genesis; both texts focus on Abraham and present him as a model of faith. The text from John is also concerned with faith, but not with Abraham. Instead we encounter Nicodemus, a religious leader, who comes to Jesus to confirm certain conclusions that some were forming as they observed Jesus. The conversation centers on second birth, but ultimately it provides the Johannine Jesus an opportunity to speak about his being "lifted up" so that those who believe in him will be saved.

The Epistle: *Romans 4:1-5, 13-17*

Believing the "Works Righteousness" Out of Lent

Setting. These verses come in the second major section of Paul's letter to the Roman Christians. This segment of the epistle runs from 3:21–4:25 and is concerned with God's revealed righteousness, which is itself saving power. The passage presents Abraham as a model for relations with God, arguing from his story that one is saved by faith in the promise of God rather than by any work(s) that one does oneself.

Structure. The lectionary omits vv. 6-12, but one may deal with all or parts of the seventeen verses (as is always the case!). Chapter 4 actually forms a complete unity of Paul's thought in Romans, but it is possible to view the lectionary text in three parts: vv. 1-8 treat the justification of Abraham by faith; vv. 9-12 make a chronological argument about the priority of faith over works by recalling how Abraham was reckoned righteous before he was circumcised; and vv. 13-17 use Abraham's story as a point of departure for reflecting upon the dynamic relationship of promise and faith. The three parts of the passage may tempt the preacher to go looking for a poem on grace or faith.

Significance. Earlier in this letter Paul claimed that God's newly revealed righteousness in Jesus Christ actually had precedence over the law and the prophets. Because he and his co-religionists (formerly Jewish, currently Christian) all believed that scripture admits one to God's truth, now the apostle turns to argue from scripture to validate his contentions. He works in an adroit manner, reaching back through Israel's history, around Moses and the law, to "Abraham, our ancestor according the the flesh" (4:1).

In vv. 2-8 Paul correlates two passages of scripture to create the perfect proof that one is saved by faith, not works. First, the apostle cites Genesis 15:6 to show that Abraham's belief in God was the occasion of his being reckoned righteous; then, he quotes Psalm 32, which uses language similar to the Genesis quotation, to pronounce a blessing on those whom the Lord forgives. Paul's style of arguing may seem strange to modern readers, but it is standard first-century Jewish scriptural interpretation. The use of Abraham as a type employs midrashic techniques to advance an argument that is validated by a correlated text from elsewhere. Paul's point is that one is saved by grace through faith—an old saw, but one that cannot be repeated often enough, because we hear this gospel and immediately try to assist God in saving us through our own good deeds. Good deeds are fine! Good deeds are important! Good deeds should be the outcome of a life transformed by Christ! But good deeds do not save! Moreover, Protestants in particular are gifted at turning "faith" itself into the single essential saving work or act of the human will. But read Paul: Abraham trusted the God who justifies the ungodly, and his faith was reckoned as righteousness (4:5). We do not believe our way into being saved, rather we are saved, and in faith we experience the riches of God's mercy.

Verses 9-12 advance Paul's argument. Abraham's experience of saving grace prior to his being circumcised shows that we do not have to do anything before God can save us. Because Abraham was reckoned righteous when he was uncircumcised, he typifies both Gentiles and Jews in relation to God. Earlier Paul wrote of the universal sinfulness of humanity (1:18–3:20), and now he speaks of the universal scope of God's grace, which is given to all humans alike—without consideration of their current religious standings.

Finally, in vv. 13-17, still focusing on Abraham, Paul gives his argument a new twist. He speaks of God's promise, which finds fulfillment through faith, not law. Those who stand in faith are the heirs to God's promise to Abraham, not those who stand on the law. Paul's argument is not anti-Jewish, but antilaw. Or better, Paul's case is propromise and profaith. The negative dimensions of Paul's comments are likely responses to those who advocate some form of law-observance in the Christian context. For preaching today, we should allow our criticisms to fall on legalists, not Jews; and, in fact, we should wonder whether we really lose Paul's point by refraining from negative polemics. Unless we are contending with legalism in our own context, we probably do Paul no disservice by laying aside the negative dimensions of his remarks.

The Gospel: *John 3:1-17*

The Necessity of Second Birth

Setting. We come in Lent to a series of four texts from the Fourth Gospel. This first text gives us a section of the story of Jesus' encounter with Nicodemus (3:1-21). The passage is filled with unique Johannine thoughts, language, ideas, and literary techniques.

In John's storytelling, Nicodemus functions as a kind of straight man for Jesus. This whole incident is crafted in one of John's favorite forms: a narrative introduces dialogue that produces misunderstanding which allows Jesus to make a long speech. Indeed, in the initial exchanges between Jesus and Nicodemus, Jesus addresses Nicodemus with the singular form of the second person pronoun, "you"; but beginning in v. 12, Jesus suddenly starts to speak to "y'all"— employing the second person plural pronoun. Nicodemus simply disappears in the narrative after he speaks in v. 9 and is addressed by Jesus in vv. 10-11. Clearly the story and the conversation are pointed toward a larger audience, which is directly addressed ("y'all") in vv. 12-17 (21).

The scene is highly symbolic. Nicodemus comes "by night"—at least as much a reference to his being in the dark as it is to the time of day. The conversation refers to (1) "signs"—an interpretation of the nature and purpose of Jesus' mighty acts (or, miracles); (2) being born *anōthen*—an ambiguous Greek word that can mean "again" or "from above"; (3) being "born of water and the Spirit"—that is, divine cleansing in the messianic age; (4) "wind and the Spirit"—a word play evoking images of divine creative activity; (5) Jesus' being "lifted up"—a complex reference to Jesus' crucifixion and exaltation; and (6) "eternal life"—a qualitative, not merely, durative existence in relation to God. Moreover, throughout the larger passage there is a steady stream of antinomic apocalyptic language: flesh/Spirit (v. 6), earth/heaven (v. 12), light/darkness (v. 13), believing/not believing (v. 18), and doing evil/doing truth (v. 21).

Structure. John begins with a narrative (vv. 1-2*a*), which rapidly

47

turns into a conversation (vv. 2*b*-11) and eventuates in Jesus' making a speech (vv. 12-21). The conversation runs through three cycles: First, Nicodemus makes a statement that Jesus (oddly) "answers" with a declaration about second birth; and Nicodemus asks, "How . . . ?" (vv. 2*b*-4). Second, Jesus gives another pronouncement-answer about second birth; and Nicodemus queries, "How . . . ?" (vv. 5-9). Third, Jesus responds with a question and an elaborate statement about "earthly things" and "heavenly things" and God's saving love, which motivated the sending of God's Son to save the world (vv. 10-17 [21]).

Significance. Poor Nicodemus follows nearly none of the symbolism in Jesus' speech! Rather, the perplexed Nicodemus is confronted at every state of his inquiry by ambiguous metaphors and enigmatic antinomies, so that his initial claims to knowledge and belief are frustrated, if not refuted. The episode reveals that Nicodemus knows nothing other than that Jesus came from God and that knowledge alone is inadequate. Yet, this is more a literary device than a historical recollection. Indeed, as Nicodemus does not comprehend, Jesus speaks more and more, so that we, the readers of the Gospel, are in the privileged position of being instructed by Jesus on a series of topics.

The first cycle of conversation declares the necessity of divinely empowered spiritual birth. Jesus says one must be born *anōthen*, and Nicodemus hears "again" rather than "from above," so that his subsequent remarks are comical, but we get the point. The second cycle elaborates the theme, teaching that entry into God's kingdom requires divinely empowered spiritual birth because like answers to like. Thus, without the movement of the Spirit in our lives, we have no means of relating to God. The third cycle clarifies the role of Jesus in salvation. At God's initiative, because of God's love, God sent or gave God's Son, who is the criterion of salvation. The presence and person of Jesus Christ forces a crisis, so that Jesus is the catalyst that precipitates a separation of "light" and "darkness," of "truth" and "evil."

The passage makes a profound statement that is highly relevant for our lives. Orthodoxy is not the key to being a Christian; rather, God expects an inseparable bonding of orthodoxy and orthopraxis, solid belief with sound practice. Eternal life is a quality of existence that has its beginning in this life in anticipation of another life. Eternal life came because of what God has done in Jesus Christ. Christians live by forming life out of a belief that Jesus guides and empowers all of existence.

Lent 2: The Celebration

It is obvious that the lesson intends faith to be the theme of the day. Preachers should be guided by the exegetical comment here, as well as by their own study. Biblical preaching will seek to define and illustrate faith in terms of the texts rather than topically or philosophically. Perhaps the primary duty of the preacher will be to open up the question of what it means for faith to be a gift from God rather than an activity performed by the devout. The exhortation to "have faith" has become its own form of works righteousness in much of Protestantism. For example, note that in the new Roman Catholic liturgy for admission to the catechumenate, those being received as catechumens are first asked, "What do you ask of God's Church?" and the response is "Faith." This makes clear that faith is a gift shared corporately, not an individual treasure to be hoarded.

Either of the following prayers from the British Methodist Service Book could serve as the opening prayer or the prayer of the day prior to the reading of the lessons.

Almighty God, your chosen servant Abraham faithfully obeyed your call and rejoiced in your promise that in him all the families of the earth should be blessed. Give us a faith like his, that in us your promises may be fulfilled; through Jesus Christ our Lord.

Almighty and ever-living God, increase in us your gift of faith that, forsaking what lies behind and reaching out to that which is before us, we may run the way of your commandments and win the crown of everlasting joy; through Jesus Christ our Lord.

There apparently are few hymns that deal with faith as gift. Two very good texts can be found in the 1964 Methodist Book of Hymns : "Father, I Stretch My Hands to Thee" (140) and "O for a Faith That Will Not Shrink" (142).

The following text by Charles Wesley refers to faith as that which God does in the soul of the believer and relates today's Lenten themes to the Paschal celebration that we are anticipating. It needs a tune with a strong common meter.

Father of Jesus Christ—my Lord,
My Savior, and my Head—
I trust in thee, whose powerful word
Has raised him from the dead.

Faith in thy power thou seest I have,
For thou this faith hast wrought;
Dead souls thou callest from their grave,
And speakest words from nought.

Faith, mighty faith, the promise sees,
And looks to that alone,
Laughs at impossibilities,
And cries, "It shall be done!"

Obedient faith, that waits on thee,
Thou never wilt reprove,
But thou wilt form thy Son in me,
And perfect me in love.

*From *Hymns and Psalms: A Methodist and Ecumenical Hymn Book* (London: Methodist Publishing House, 1983), no. 693.

Third Sunday in Lent

Old Testament Texts

The central theme of the Old Testament texts can be stated as a question: Is the Lord in our midst or not? The central motif that is used to answer the question in Exodus 17:1-7 is the miraculous gift of water in the wilderness. This motif links the Old Testament lesson and the gospel text for this Sunday. Psalm 95 provides commentary on the wilderness story from a somewhat different direction. As we will see, the account of Israel's testing God in the wilderness is not a negative story in its present narrative setting. Israel tests God, and God provides water, which answers the central question about whether or not God is in fact with the people. The hymn in Psalm 95, however, shifts the setting from the wilderness to worship and in so doing interprets Exodus 17:1-7 negatively, as though it is cautioning us about testing the presence of God in the midst of worship itself.

The Lesson: *Exodus 17:1-7*

Is the Lord in Our Midst or Not?

Setting. Exodus 17:1-7 is one of the early wilderness stories. The Lord has delivered Israel from Egypt in Exodus 15, and the once enslaved people now have the responsibility of political freedom, but without the benefit of a country, because the Lord frees Israel into the wilderness. As the lesson makes very clear, this is a mixed blessing, for it means that Israel is still a people at risk. In many ways, their enslavement to Egypt has really become an enslavement to God, for just as they could not live without Egyptian favor in Egypt, so now they cannot live without divine favor in the wilderness. Their new enslavement becomes all too clear when the water runs out in the midst of the desert. The crisis simply underscores how this first wilderness generation is a people in training. Exodus 17:1-7 raises the question of how the people of God conform to the risks of their new enslavement. They test God with the question: Is God in our midst or not?

Structure. Verses 1-2 include an itinerary notice (an account of the places to which Israel journeyed in the wilderness) and an initial confrontation between the people and Moses about the lack of water. The remainder of the story separates into four parts. It begins with a quotation from the people questioning the purpose of salvation in the light of their present dilemma (v. 3). The second section shifts the focus to Moses, who turns the matter over to God (v. 4). The Lord enters the story in vv. 5-6*a* in response to Moses' request. And the episode ends with Moses following the directions of God for drawing water from a rock and with a narrator providing a concluding summary.

Significance. Exodus 17:1-7 is one of the murmuring stories. These stories are a series of accounts in Exodus and Numbers in which Israel complains about a threat in the wilderness (for example, lack of water or food). These stories become very negative as we read along in the Pentateuch until finally they become illustrations of Israel's lack of faith in God. For example, Exodus 17:1-7 repeats in Numbers 20, where the drawing of water from the rock of Meribah illustrates the disobedience of both Moses and the people. Even though the murmuring stories evolve into negative stories about Israel, it would be a mistake to read all of them that way, especially the early stories like Exodus 17:1-7. The first account of Israel at Meribah/Massah is less a story about Israel's lack of faith, than it is about whether God is in fact with the people.

This early murmuring story is constructed around questions. The newly liberated Israelites barely finish their song of celebration in Exodus 15:1-21 before they are confronted with the unknown risks of the wilderness. At this point they lack both place and identity. The early wilderness stories are meant to address the latter problem, by probing the question of what salvation now means for the people. Israel's confrontation with Moses in v. 3, "Did we go up from Egypt simply to die?" is such a question. As the story continues it becomes apparent that Moses is of no help in answering this question. He deftly turns the question over to God in v. 4, "What shall I do?" Finally, Israel's question is answered by God, who directs Moses to draw water from a rock. The miraculous drawing of water from the rock states at least two things about the nature of Israel's salvation: first, they were not liberated for death in the wilderness; and, second, liberation is transferred dependency from Egypt to God. Given that salvation is not independence, there is a proper time to test God, and Exodus 17:1-7 provides an illustration of such a time. The story concludes with a narrator naming the location as Meribah and Massah. These are Hebrew words meaning "to present a legal case against someone" (Meribah) and "to test" (Massah). The RSV translation of the verbal form of Meribah in v. 7 as "because of the faultfinding of . . . " is too negative and it has been changed in the NRSV to read, "because the Israelites quarreled and tested the LORD."

Too often we do not allow for doubt in the contemporary Church. One wonders if the reason for this is that God is not real enough for us in this skeptical age to withstand any doubting. Whatever our reasons for not testing God, this story makes it clear that there is a proper place for doubt, and this should be emphasized in preaching this text. Thus the issue in this story is not to judge Israel negatively as lacking faith, but to raise the question concerning the reliability of God. That is why the story ends with the question, "Is the LORD among us or not?" The placing of the question by Israel was appropriate, and the answer in the light of the story is yes.

The Response: *Psalm 95*

Affirming the Presence of God

Setting. Psalm 95 includes a combination of elements that make the psalm stand out. It includes a call to praise God and reasons for praise, which are common to the hymn form. Then it concludes with a form that is more like a prophetic oracle than a hymn, which then shifts over into divine discourse in order to interpret the wilderness stories of Meribah and Massah negatively.

Structure. Psalm 95 separates into three parts that can be outlined as follows:

   I. A Call to Praise with Reason for Praise
      A. A Call to Praise (vv. 1-2)
      B. Reason for Praise (vv. 3-5)
  II. A Call to Praise with Reason for Praise
      A. A Call to Praise (v. 6)
      B. Reason for Praise (v. 7*a*)
 III. A Call to Faithfulness with Reason
      A. A Call to Faithfulness (v. 7*b*)
      B. Reason for Faithfulness (vv. 8-11)

Significance. Psalm 95 provides a qualification of our interpretation of Exodus 17:1-7. If the message of Exodus 17:1-7 suggests that there is an appropriate time to test the presence of God, the message of Psalm 95 suggests the reverse—namely, that there are also times when we don't test the presence of God. The conclusion of Psalm 95 is that worship is one of those occasions where the presence of God must not be doubted. The first two strophes are hymnic calls to worship God, which explore the power of God as creator and savior as the reason for praising God. The setting of this call to praise is within the worshiping community. The motifs within these two strophes illustrate how closely they are tied together. The call to praise in the first strophe uses the language of salvation, "let us make a joyful noise to the rock of our salvation." The reasons for celebrating the salvific power of God in vv. 3-5 have to do with God's creative power. The second strophe moves in the opposite direction. It presents a call to worship God as creator (v. 6), but then gives reasons for such praise based on God's ability to save. The third strophe underscores how the power of God need not and indeed must not be tested in the context of worship. Worship is not the wilderness.

The first generation of Israelites in the wilderness becomes negative examples in the light of the message of Psalm 95. They become idealized in the psalm as those who are unable to enter God's sanctuary, because they were unable to move beyond testing God. This interpretation goes beyond Exodus 17:1-7 and includes Numbers

20, where the story repeats. The murmuring for water in Numbers 20 at the end of the wilderness period is one of the reasons why this generation and even Moses their leader were unable to enter the promised land of rest. The motif of "entering" (Hebrew, *bw'*) carries this meaning within the psalm. Note how the second call to praise in v. 6 is an invitation "to enter" (Hebrew, *bw'*) the sanctuary to worship. The closing line of the psalm provides a negative counterpoint to this invitation by reminding the worshipers that inappropriate testing kept the wilderness generation from "entering God's rest." The message of the psalm is that worship is not the wilderness, and to test God in worship is to harden our hearts to the presence of God that first drew us into the sanctuary. But the message of the psalm does not negate the message of Exodus 17:1-7; indeed, there will be wilderness periods when we must have the faith to test God's reliability. And especially at those times, worship must become an oasis for us.

New Testament Texts

Romans presents a tough piece of Pauline theology in the form of a meditation on justification. By contrast, the passage from John is a beautiful, elaborate narrative that is at least as sophisticated as Paul's statements, but much easier to read through. Both texts are complex, however, and require careful attention.

The Epistle: *Romans 5:1-11*

Our New Standing with God

Setting. The dominant concern of chapters 5–8 is the life of the Christian community, especially in its experience of grace. The foregoing chapters were concerned with the righteousness of God and the sin of humankind, Jews and Gentiles, law and faith; and these themes were developed through a series of exegetical arguments. A turn from theological juxtapositions and exegetical explanations began in 4:23-25; and now in chapter 5 we find Paul meditating overtly on the nature and significance of Christian existence in this world. The previous polemic and dialectic yields to an essentially straightforward (for Paul!) celebration of grace.

Structure. The passage has two complementary parts. Verses 1-5 declare our (let us stand with the Romans and not at a distance) justification and expand upon that theme, and vv. 6-11 elucidate the meaning of Jesus Christ's death for our lives. In both parts there is a certain linear logic: First, justification means we have grace and hope, and Paul sketches a line of practical progress from the present (grace) to the future (hope). Second, Christ's death for us as sinners means our present justification and our future salvation—all of which is "reconciliation."

Significance. One is sorely tempted to do a series of word studies in relation to this passage, since it is loaded with significant theological terminology. Such a tactic may unpack much of the meaning of this text, but it will also render Paul's thinking fairly static, whereas in fact he is expressing the dynamic quality of Christian life in these verses. Thus we need to create a sense of motion that will impart some of Paul's own energy to our congregations when reflecting on this passage.

Paul starts with the present, saying that we are justified by faith (literally, Paul speaks spatially, not instrumentally, saying "we are justified out of faith"). Being justified in theological terms is like being justified in typing or printing; it means that everything has been set into a proper line. Christians are neither ragged-right nor ragged-left, we are justified. Actually, we have been justified because God has set us into the right relationship with God's self through Jesus Christ. Thus, our justification is grace! This good news puts us at peace, because, Paul says, we have (through being justified) access to grace. But this experience of the goodness of God is neither static nor complete! For the apostle immediately talks of our hope. Hope is related to our future, which has been created by the gracious work of God in Jesus Christ. For Paul, this scheme is far from "possibility thinking"; rather, it is "reality living." So Paul continues his 0meditation by bringing us all down into the swamps of life—suffering. Yet look how Paul can speak of suffering. He does not deny its reality.

He does not glorify it. Instead he puts a good face on it by relating it to endurance and character-building. Oddly, the outcome of our suffering, which produces endurance and builds character, is that we hope.

Paul has taken us for a ride in a logical loop: We rejoice in our hope allowing us to rejoice in our suffering, which yields endurance and increases character and produces hope. Christian existence, created by grace, is set in motion after hope, which is not yet fully realized but which is already present in a preliminary way. Paul says we live as we do because God's own love is poured into our hearts by the Holy Spirit.

Paul continues by speaking of our past. He says we were weak. By this he means that we were formerly ungodly—we were sinners. But perhaps because he has already devoted significant attention to our sinfulness, Paul does not ponder that matter here. Instead, with the time and space of our ungodly past evoked, Paul drops God's saving work in Jesus Christ into our midst. Then we move back to the present, and Paul once again declares our current status by saying that now we are justified by the death of Jesus Christ. The apostle is not interested in explaining how Christ's death justifies us; rather, he brings in this idea to remark on the marvelously unmerited character of God's love. Though we did not deserve it, God's love is so great that it did for us what we could not do for ourselves—it justified us!

Paul does not stop in the present; instead he casts his eyes toward the future once again and says that we will be saved by Christ's life (a reference to his Resurrection). It is instructive to notice that Paul thinks of the death of Christ in relation to current earthly Christian existence, but he speaks of the Resurrection of Christ in relation to believers' future heavenly life. For Paul, the glory of the present is the glory of the cross, and the glory of the future, which is our hope, is the glory of the Resurrection. The two are inseparably linked, but Paul does not conflate them. As the apostle distinguishes the present from the future, he holds the two together (with the future actually giving meaning to the present) by bringing everything under the rubric of "reconciliation." For Paul, reconciliation is an all-pervasive theological reality created through the many dimensions of God's work in and through Jesus Christ.

The Gospel: *John 4:5-42*

The Slaking of Spiritual Thirst

Setting. Ancient Palestinian history helps us understand this wonderful story of Jesus and the Samaritan woman. Samaritans were descendants of the Israelites of the Northern Kingdom who had intermarried with non-Jews of the region. They revered only the Pentateuch and denied the centrality of the Jerusalem Temple, having their own temple on Mount Gerizim. There was friction between Jews and Samaritans from the time of the return of the captives from the Babylonian exile (fifth century B.C.E.), and about a century before Christ, the Jews had razed the Samaritans' temple.

Structure. Initially this story is structured much like the one of Jesus and Nicodemus: narrative leads to conversation, which is filled with misunderstanding, but there is much more here as scenes and characters come and go. Generally, the story is skillfully constructed along the lines of Greek drama, wherein no more than two speaking characters appear at once though multitudes stand in the background as a chorus. Such construction says nothing about historicity, but it shows John's consummate artistry as a story-teller/writer.

Significance. This passage is about the gradual self-revelation of the identity of Jesus Christ. Through the long, enigmatic, even twisted conversation, the woman, and in turn her fellow Samaritans, perceive who Jesus really is. Initially she sees that Jesus is "a Jew" (4:9); then, she calls him "Lord" (4:11)—though with little comprehension; next, she asks whether he is "greater than our ancestor Jacob" (4:12); and after he reveals his knowledge of her past, she calls him "a prophet" (4:19); but, finally she stands with all the Samaritan townspeople as they confess him to be "the savior of the world" (4:42).

Jesus is a Jew, but he strikes the Samaritan woman as a most unusual Jew. He surprises her by stepping across the line of ethnic hostility to approach her as any other human being. Indeed, he assumes an inferior position when he asks her for a favor. Later in the story (2:27) he strikes his own disciples as an unusual Jew, because they find him talking freely with a woman—something thought to be beneath a Jewish man's dignity at the time.

As the conversation unwinds, the woman does not follow Jesus as he speaks in theological metaphors about the saving gift of life. Remarkably, Jesus is not harsh with her as he was with Nicodemus. She has claimed no knowledge, and indeed could not be expected to grasp the lofty level of Jesus' statements—though we as readers certainly should follow the turns of the conversation from our privileged position. The woman calls Jesus *kyrios* which may mean no more than "Sir" when set on her lips, but which should certainly remind Christian readers that Jesus is "Lord." The woman does not yet perceive Jesus' true identity, but nevertheless she recognizes his dignity as she courteously continues the conversation.

Jesus takes the initiative in revealing himself to this woman by challenging her to call her husband. The point here is not pedagogy or pastoral care, but provocative theology. Neither John's story nor Jesus takes an interest in the woman's seemingly sordid past; instead, Jesus brings it up to demonstrate his prophetic capacities. The woman perceives his abilities, and this stimulates further dialogue about the religious differences between the Samaritans and the Jews. Jesus uses the stated differences as a springboard to talk in eschatological terms about God's future, which will eliminate such distinctions in the unification of spirit and truth.

The woman now takes the turn with Jesus and speaks eschatologically of the coming of the Messiah. Again, this sets up Jesus' self-disclosure, "I who am speaking with you am he." But the story does not stop here. Through the following episodes Jesus speaks about proper spiritual priorities, before he finally comes into direct contact with the Samaritan townsfolk. The woman told the others about Jesus, and they initially believed upon the basis of her testimony (apparently that he was the Messiah), but after their encounter with Jesus himself they say, "It is no longer because of what you have said that we believe, for we have heard for ourselves, and we know that this is truly the Savior of the world." The position at which these people arrive is indeed where John holds all believers should be—in truth, knowing personally that Jesus is Savior, and thereby having life in his name.

Lent 3: The Celebration

Today's texts with their emphasis on water are intended to point us towards Easter and a consideration of the meaning of baptism. Here is an occasion for doctrinal preaching as the preacher relates the scripture to his or her denomination's official teaching about the meaning of baptism. Such preaching should also lead the hearers to identify their baptismal experience with the scriptural witness.

The preacher is challenged by this pairing of texts to deal with a typological exposition. Such a method of interpreting scripture was very popular in the early Church (see I Cor. 10:1-4 for Paul's use of it in relation to today's Exodus lesson) and in the preaching of the patristic age. St. Ambrose writes concerning I Corinthians 10:

> "They drank from the supernatural Rock which followed them, and the Rock was Christ." Drink, you too, that Christ may follow along with you. See the mystery! Moses is the prophet; his staff is God's word. The priest [Moses] touches the rock with the word of God and water flows, and the people drink. So, too, the priest [in the Eucharist] touches the chalice and water flows in the chalice and leaps up for eternal life. [quoted in Nocent, II, p. 95]

Typological preaching came under suspicion with the advent of the scholarly scientific-historical method and was frequently derided as "seeing Jesus behind every rock in the Old Testament." The intent of such preaching is not to see "the little man who wasn't there"; rather, it is to view the text with the eyes of faith and not as a historical critic alone, to think in images rather than in static linear categories. Imaginative preaching is preaching with images rather than concepts; it is preaching aimed more at seeing than understanding.

A doctrinal sermon about baptism based on these texts can be something more than a set of abstract propositions about what baptism means and what the faithful must believe about it. It will illustrate the faithfulness of God in the face of our unfaithfulness; it will help us experience again the mystery of that grace which was extended to us "while we were yet helpless" and "in which we stand."

Today's service might place the confession of sin after the Old Testament lesson, using a prayer that deals corporately with our lack of faith and contemporary murmuring. The absolution or words of assurance might then include a sprinkling of water towards the congregation, using the formula that may have been employed earlier on Ash Wednesday: "God will cast all our sins into the depths of the sea," and so liturgically anticipating the Exodus narrative, which will be read at Easter. Psalm 95 then becomes a response of thanksgiving to the absolution. To respond to the reading of the Gospel, use from "Glorious Things of Thee Are Spoken" the stanza that begins "See, the streams of living waters."

Fourth Sunday in Lent

Old Testament Texts

The Old Testament texts explore what it means to be anointed by God. I Samuel 16:1-13 is the account of the anointing of David by Samuel and Psalm 23 is a prayer song in which the worshiper who has experienced threatening events also experiences the security of God through anointing. I Samuel 16:1-13 highlights the risks that accompany the anointing of God, while Psalm 23 outlines the unique security that God offers each of us.

The Lesson: *I Samuel 16:1-13*

The Risk of Anointing

Setting. I Samuel 16:1-13 is about the anointing of David. An overview of the larger context of I Samuel will illustrate how this story plays an important transitional role in the larger account of Saul and David and how David's anointing puts him on a risk-filled journey. In I Samuel 8, Saul is anointed to be the first leader of Israel, and for eight chapters, the reader follows his rise in power until I Samuel 15, which marks his downfall. I Samuel 16 begins with a motif of mourning when God asks Samuel how long he will lament the fall of Saul. The implied answer to the question is that he should not be mourning Saul at all, because there is a new king who must be anointed. The command for Samuel to "fill his horn with oil" introduces the central motif of our Old Testament lesson, since the goal of this story is for Samuel to discover and to anoint this new king. With the anointing of David, I Samuel becomes a story of his rise and Saul's decline. (Note the contrast between v. 13 and v. 14—the Spirit of God simultaneously descends on David and departs from Saul.) As any reader of I Samuel knows, however, the rise of David is filled with risk. He is anointed into a whirlwind of threats by a giant, by Saul, by enemy nations, and so on. His only security is the promise of God's protection.

Structure. I Samuel 16:1-13 separates into three parts, each of which includes a divine speech to Samuel and an account of Samuel's obedient response. The text can be outlined in the following manner:

> I. The Command to Anoint a New King (vv. 1-5)
>   A. The First Divine Command and Response by Samuel
>   (The risk of anointing a new king)
>   B. The Obedience of Samuel (vv. 4-5)
> II. The Search for a New King (vv. 6-11)
>   A. Samuel's Choice and the Second Divine Command (vv. 6-7)
>   (The problem of perception)
>   B. The Obedience of Samuel (vv. 8-11)
> III. The Anointing (vv. 12-13)
>   A. The Third Divine Command (v. 12)
>   B. The Obedience of Samuel (v. 13)

Significance. Even though the central theme of this text is about the anointing of David in order to introduce his important role in the remainder of the book, nevertheless, the outline underscores how Samuel—rather than David—is really the central character within the story itself. Thus Samuel deserves our attention in exploring the importance of anointing, because in many ways his role within the story illustrates many of the risk-filled aspects of David's anointing that will be played out in the larger structure of I Samuel.

The risks to Samuel in anointing of David are stated clearly in his first response to God in v. 2: "How can I go? If Saul hears of it, he will kill me." God's response to Samuel is that he must take a heifer for sacrificing (supposedly as a ruse to Saul), and then God would point out the future king during the sacrifice. The first scene closes with the narrator underscoring Samuel's faithfulness. Yet God's closing promise that he would point out the new king to Samuel provides the stage for Samuel's next problem, namely how to choose between

Jesse's sons. Samuel immediately picks Eliab (presumably because he is the most striking in appearance), prompting the divine caution that God's anointing is not in response to outward appearance. Instead "the Lord looks on the heart." Once again Samuel is obedient to God's directions, and thus he continues the search through all Jesse's sons. The final scene opens with the divine command in v. 12 that Samuel anoint the child David, which Samuel does in v. 13, prompting an unleashing of the Spirit of God.

When using this text, the preacher may want to underscore that there are obstacles in being anointed by God and in trying to carry out God's command to anoint. David embodies the former and Samuel the latter. The obstacles to both characters, however, are very similar. There is risk because the power of God's anointing frequently is at odds with our notions of power. David will learn this lesson successfully when confronting the giant Goliath and then fail at it when he exploits the power to rule in the affair with Bathsheba (II Sam. 11). Samuel is successful in our lesson only because he learns to follow God even against his own best judgments.

The Response: *Psalm 23*

The Security of Anointing

Setting. This is one of the most familiar psalms in scripture. We all learn it as children, and over time the pastoral imagery of God as our shepherd becomes almost romantic. This is unfortunate, because even though Psalm 23 is about security, it is not a romantic psalm. In fact, the psalmist is seeking security in the midst of terror. Danger is looming large for the singer of this prayer song. Verse 4 provides the setting, and it includes images of death and evil.

Structure. The preacher has an alternative for the outline of the psalm. It could be separated into three parts: vv. 1-2, confession of God as shepherd; vv. 3-4, a description of the wanderer; and vv. 5-6, a description of God as host. But in this outline vv. 3-4 are not necessarily a description of wandering as much as they are a description of a threat. In view of this, a two-part division might better convey the message of the psalm: vv. 1-4, a confession of God as shepherd in the context of a threat; and vv. 5-6, a confession of divine security in the context of the worshiping community.

Significance. The significance of Psalm 23 is in the contrast between the two parts, which underscores the security of God's anointing. The first section of the psalm divides between a description of God as shepherd in vv. 1-3 and the situation of the psalmist in v. 4. God is a shepherd, who is able to lead, restore, and provide nurture (vv. 1-3), even in the darkest situations (v. 4), because he is never absent from us. Note that the only direct address to God in vv. 1-4 occurs in v. 4 ("For you are with me."). This confession underscores how God is present even when we have moved to the outer reaches of God's domain and thus come under the shadow of death. The scene changes abruptly, however, in vv. 5-6 from circumstances of threat and death to a banquet, as the worshiper moves into the very presence of God within the sanctuary. Here the metaphors for God shift from shepherd in a threatening situation to host within the security of a home. God prepares a banquet for worshiper and enemies. This shift in imagery from shepherd to host underscores how worship is where our real security lies. As one commentator on this psalm states, worship is the sphere where God's protection is most readily available. This reality is underscored through the motif of anointing in v. 5, which gives rise to a whole new perspective on the part of the worshiper. The threat of enemies in pursuit through a valley of death shifts in v. 6 to the pursuit of goodness and mercy in the temple of God—even while the enemies look on. The confession of the worshiper in v. 6 is anything but a romantic vision, for it goes against our notions of security.

David, Samuel, and the psalmist underscore how the baptism of God puts us on a high-risk road that forces us to live our lives under the hospitality of God's protection, which, the psalmist reminds us, is the only place where security lies for any circumstance.

New Testament Texts

These passages are united in their common use of symbolic language of night/day or darkness/light for speaking of God's will and what sits in opposition to it. Ephesians addresses Christian behavior of the time but affirms Christ's crucial role in that existence. John is primarily interested in Christology, but the story has rich implication for the way that Christians perceive their lives.

The Epistle: *Ephesians 5:8-14*

Practical Words on Christian Life

Setting. Ephesians is shaped like a normal Pauline letter, but upon examination one finds this writing to be quite different from the other letters attributed to Paul in the New Testament. There is a salutation in 1:1-2 and a lofty doxological statement in 1:3-14 where one would expect a thanksgiving-prayer report. The remainder of chapter 1 and chapters 2 and 3 present sublime theological reflections. Then in chapters 4–6, one finds fairly mundane directions for everyday Christian life laced with theological metaphors. The passage for this week from Ephesians 5 is an excellent example of this combination.

Structure. The passage begins with the negative memory of the readers' sinful past and moves quickly to the positive reality of their current Christian life (v. 8a). Having contrasted the old and the new life, the passage continues with a series of three admonitions: (1) Live as children of light (v. 8b); (2) try to find out what is pleasing to the Lord (v. 10); and (3) take no part in evil, rather expose it (v. 11). The passage elaborates these points by giving reasons for following the directions given. Finally, the passage ends by quoting what appears to be an early Christian hymn, perhaps based on Isaiah 60:1 (v. 14).

Significance. This passage is fairly straightforward. The metaphorical contrast between good and evil, or God's will and what opposes it, employs familiar light/darkness language. Ancients commonly used this vocabulary, and in the circles of Judaism from 200 B.C.E. to 100 C.E., such terms became the technical terminology of apocalyptic eschatological teaching. Christianity inherited such language from its environment.

For moderns reading or hearing this text, the only problem will be a tendency to simply think in terms of good and bad behavior. This biblical language speaks of far more than that. It is cosmological and theological in nature. Notice that v. 14 says Christ shines on the one who is redeemed. Darkness and light are thought of as realms and forces set in powerful opposition to each other. The author and other ancients believed that humanity lives in one or the other of these realms and under the influence of the power of that realm. Today, people do not think in such terms—at least not most folks in Protestant congregations; so what are we to do to preach this text with integrity?

The author gives us a clue. Sometimes it is helpful in our current Christian context to recall how things were before our priorities were established as a result of our confession of the lordship of Jesus Christ. Other forces shaped us. Perhaps it was pure selfishness, greed, or a desire for power or security. Whatever it was, it was indeed a force larger than we ourselves, and it had control of our lives, so that we were not free. A life in Christ is altered, not perfected, but different from before its rebirth in Christ. As we stand in the Christian present, thinking about our lives before Christ, we can hear the author's admonitions to pursue God's good desires, to abstain from what is not in keeping with God's revealed love—even giving ourselves to oppose it. We live in Christ as Christians simply because Christ has claimed us in love.

All of the reflection above can be illustrated in relation to the particular situations we face in our congregations and in our local communities. We may also follow the lead of Ephesians and "kick up" the level of our reflection to the heights. Matters of national and international significance, the roles that other Christians are playing at home and around the world in standing for justice and mercy, and against oppression and intolerance, all provide illustrations that can assist us in making this passage heard today.

The Gospel: *John 9:1-41*

Sight for One Born Blind

Setting. The first half of John is often called "The Book of Signs," because it recounts several acts of Jesus that are designated "signs"—meaning, they point beyond the striking deeds to the true identity of Jesus. These stories are thought to have had a life prior to their incorporation into the current context of the gospel, and they are often large and essentially free-standing narratives. John 9 is a beautifully constructed unit, capable of standing alone, and containing in it practically all the essentials of the gospel as John declares it.

Structure. On the surface John 9 has the form of a "miracle story." One may profitably compare it with the healings of blind Bartimaeus (Mark 10:46-52 and parallels) and of the blind man of Bethsaida (Mark 8:22-26). As in those other gospel stories and other ancient miracle stories, one finds the healing account has three parts: a description of the sickness, the act of healing, and some confirmation of the miracle—the person demonstrates health or the onlookers are amazed. But in John 9 there is much more. The healing is "set up" by the disciples' question (v. 2) and Jesus' speech-answer (vv. 3-5). Remarkably Jesus drops out of the story after v. 7 and does not reappear until v. 35. And all the material in vv. 8-41 is dramatic expansion building off the basic miracle story. The text has been analyzed by several scholars (most notably by J. Louis Martyn in *History and Theology in the Fourth Gospel* [revised edition; Nashville: Abingdon, 1979], pp. 24-36). It comprises seven carefully constructed scenes: (1) Jesus, his disciples, and the blind man (vv. 1-7); (2) the blind man and his neighbors (vv. 8-12); (3) the blind man and the Pharisees (vv. 13-17); (4) the Pharisees and the blind man's parents (vv. 18-23); (5) the Pharisees and the blind man (vv. 24-34); (6) Jesus and the blind man (vv. 35-38); and (7) Jesus and the Pharisees (vv. 39-41). Any one or more of these scenes could be the text for a sermon.

Significance. The main concern of this story as a whole is the articulation of Christology, similar to the thrust of the story of Jesus and the Samaritan woman. This story holds a special place in the gospel, however, for scholars conclude that in this account we have rich testimony to the evolution of Christology in the Johannine community. In the story of the healed blind-born man, one finds a dramatic recapitulation of the plight of the members of John's community, or church, who had themselves been evicted from the synagogue, as is the healed man in this story (see vv. 22, 34). Recast in this story, especially in vv. 8-41, is the story of the growth of the early Johannine church's understanding of Jesus, so that the larger miracle account becomes a vehicle for declaring the identity of Jesus Christ. In brief, the story of the growth of christological insight within this expanded miracle story is this: Originally, Christ is recognized only as "the man called Jesus" (v. 11). But in the light of his power in ministry, it is understood that "he is a prophet" (v. 17). In turn, believing Jews confess that Jesus is "the Christ" (v. 22), but this produces a division—with some saying he is "from God" (v. 33), while others contend he is not from God because he is "a sinner" (v. 24). Jesus himself teaches that he is "the Son of Man" (v. 35)—throughout John this title is associated with Jesus' death, Resurrection, Ascension, and gift of the Spirit. Ultimately, we hear the confession that Jesus is "Lord" (v. 38)—a title connoting that he is the Son of God and the preexistent, creative Word.

A quick walk through the scenes will allow us to see the plethora of theological themes in this narrative:

Sin. In vv. 1-7 we encounter the issue of the relation of sin and sickness. But Jesus refuses to play the blame-game and speaks instead of the will of God in relation to ministry to those who suffer. Because the blind man is obedient to Jesus, he receives his sight. Notice that the man was born blind—meaning, created imperfectly—and Jesus makes mud, just as God formed clay to create humanity.

Transformation. In vv. 8-12 we observe the obvious change in the man, but we find that his newly altered perspective does not endow him with full comprehension. Thus we learn that conversion is not an end in itself.

Sabbath. In vv. 13-17 we come upon another classic New Testament form, a Sabbath-controversy. The Pharisees are cast as the religious authorities of the day, likely an anachronism. There is, however, a division among them, and the outcome is a minimal confession (of Jesus as prophet) on the part of the formerly blind man.

Fear. In vv. 18-23 "the Jews" (as if all in this story were not Jews!) quiz the blind man's parents. Under fire, the parents protest too much. They were asked three questions, but they answer four—going on to deny they know "who" healed their son—out of fear of expulsion from the synagogue for confessing Jesus as Christ.

Expulsion. In vv. 24-35, through a heated discussion between the Pharisees and the healed man, we learn of the contrast between disciples of Moses and disciples of Jesus, now mutually exclusive groups. "The Jews" finally answer the question that the disciples asked Jesus at the beginning of the story, declaring that the man was born in sin and expelling him from the synagogue!

Revelation. In vv. 35-38 Jesus reveals himself. This illustrates the crucial role of revelation in Christian tradition. Christ's self-disclosure brings the man to profound faith, confession, and worship.

Judge. Finally, in 9:39-41 we see Jesus, the Son of Man, cast in his role as Judge (the sense of the title "Son of Man" in Jewish literature). As Judge he acts in eschatological fashion, giving sight to the blind and blinding those who claim to see but who oppose God's work.

Lent 4: The Celebration

The Old Testament lesson and the Gospel share the common image of anointing: David is anointed by Samuel, and the blind man is anointed by Jesus. This is part of the ongoing series of lessons designed to prepare persons to receive baptism or to renew their baptismal vows at Easter. This will seem strange to many in Protestant traditions until they learn that anointing with oil has been part of the baptismal practice of many Christians. The lessons can help introduce the practice, which is now an optional part of the baptismal service in several Protestant churches.

The point of the Old Testament lesson is to emphasize that our baptismal anointing, like David's, makes us a part of a royal priesthood (I Pet. 2:9); it is a sign of our chosenness. The Queen of England, at her coronation, was dressed in priestly garments and anointed with oil. We are no less royalty and priests because of our baptism, our coronation as Christians. The above commentary can lead the preacher to explore the meaning of "the risks of baptism," the consequences of commitment. It may also lead to reflection by the pastor on the issue of "whom do I baptize?" As Samuel was at risk as the anointer, so may the pastor be at risk in pretending to more sacramental authority than God has given. The outcry over indiscriminate baptism is certainly justified, but may it need to be tempered by remembering that God alone can look on the heart? Is not grace by its very nature indiscriminate? This issue may certainly be appropriate for discussion by pastors who discuss the lectionary together in weekly sessions, even if it may not be appropriate for preaching.

The anointing in the Gospel leads to sight, to the light that is the subject of the epistle. Thus the three lessons are tied together and we are reminded that in the ancient tradition of the Church, baptism was frequently referred to as "illumination."

The Psalm 23 is chosen for the response because of its reference to anointing (v. 5). Verses 4 and 6 help us anticipate the coming of the Passion and the Resurrection. Worship planners might consider that there are several metrical arrangements of this psalm, any one of which could be used as a response to the Old Testament lesson. Six can be found in *The Presbyterian Hymnal* (1990); most standard hymnals will have at least two.

Because the Gospel so vividly depicts the blind man's movement into faith, concluding with his affirmation, "I believe," today's liturgy may significantly include the recitation of one of the historic creeds as a response to the Gospel or to the sermon.

Fifth Sunday in Lent

Old Testament Texts

The two Old Testament texts for the Fifth Sunday in Lent provide stark contrasts between death and life. Ezekiel 37:1-14 is the eerie story of the dried and wind-blown bones that spring back into life as though we were watching a movie backwards. Psalm 130 is a penitential prayer.

The Lesson: *Ezekiel 37:1-14*

Can Bones Be Brought Back to Life?

Setting. The primary setting of the book of Ezekiel is the exile. The prophetic oracles and visions in the book are addressed to a displaced people, who have lost their land, livelihood, national identity, and, most seriously of all, their faith. Their God, after all, had promised them life in the land as the fulfillment of the salvation that was wrought out of the Exodus. In exile they now find themselves to be a wilderness people. Unlike the first generation in the wilderness, the exiles are not on the move to a promised land, but just the reverse. In their experience, they are moving away from the land. It is as though they are forgotten characters in a movie where the main drama has already been played out. The exiles are hopeless anti-heroes. Ezekiel 1–32 presents judgment oracles against Israel and the nations in an attempt to explain how such a hopeless situation could have come about. Ezekiel 33–48 takes up the more difficult task of raising the question of whether the situation is, in fact, hopeless. The question that provides the overarching problem for the latter section of the book is stated by the exiles in Ezekiel 33:10, "How then can we live?" The story of the dry bones is an important part of God's answer.

Structure. Ezekiel 37:1-14 can be outlined in four sections.

I. The Setting of the Wilderness and Dry Bones (vv. 1-2)
II. The Opening Question of God to the Prophet (v. 3)
III. The Power of the Divine Word (vv. 4-10)
    A. To the Bones (vv. 4-8)
    B. To the Spirit (vv. 9-10)
IV. The Interpretation of the Bones and God's Answer to the Opening Question (vv. 11-14)

Significance. The setting is important for an interpretation of the story. Outside of the promised land Israel is a dead people—not because they have lost national identity but because they are cut off from God, whose presence is tied to Jerusalem and by extension to the land (see the discussion in *Preaching the Revised Common Lectionary*, Year A, First Sunday of Advent). In view of this reality, the answer to the question noted above, "How then can we live?" is that exiles cannot live. The opening question to the prophet in v. 3 and the prophet's evasive response simply confirm this answer. When God asks the prophet whether dried bones can be brought back to life, note how the prophet never answers, and, instead, defers the question back to God. The equivocal answer of the prophet goes to the heart of this text. From the prophet's perspective, the "you-know" response is easily interpreted as an attempt to avoid the obvious—of course dried bones cannot come back to life. Yet by attempting to avoid the obvious, the prophet does indeed place the answer to the question where it should be and that is with God rather than ourselves. The remainder of the story is God's surprising answer to the question.

Verses 4-10 present a two-part drama to demonstrate the power of the divine word. First, the prophet is commanded to preach to the bones. The power of this word inaugurates the miracle of God rev⸱ ⸱ng time before the eyes of the prophet. The wind-blown bones are ⸱ ⸱ivated, and then muscle, skin, and flesh fill out the skeletons. The imagery here is so graphic that it is the section of the story that most of us recall first. But this is not yet the final point of the story. Second, note how this episode concludes in v. 8 with the prophet telling us that there is no life. The conclusion suggests that God's bending or even reversing of time itself isn't enough. Life requires the spirit of God, which becomes the object of the second divine command to the prophet in vv. 9-10.

The spirit of the Lord is a central motif in the story, occurring no less than 10 times in fourteen verses. God tells the prophet in vv. 5, 6, 9, 10, 14 that it is the spirit which gives life. The miracle of this story is not simply that God can reverse time but that the spirit of God can give the people life even in the wilderness. Exilic Israel did not think that this was possible, for they thought that God was tied to the Jerusalem Temple and the land. God's two-part miracle is an answer to the assumptions of exiled Israelites, who are quoted in v. 11 as saying, "Our bones are dried up, and our hope is lost; we are cut off completely." The point of the story is that God has left the land to be with God's people in the wilderness of the exile. The result of God's surprising decision is that it allows the movie of the exile to be reversed. No longer are these people anti-heroes who are moving away from the land and from the presence of God. Rather, with God leaving the land to journey with Israel, the people once again acquire direction and hope, because God is now able to lead them back to the promised land of rest. For the prophet Ezekiel this is no less than a resurrection story. In preaching this text it may be helpful to explore situations or persons in your community where there is consensus that all hope is gone. The power of this text is that it is a bold statement that God is able to reverse such situations—to play them backwards—and to breathe new life into the characters.

The Response: *Psalm 130*

The Language of Hope

Setting. The penitential prayer of Psalm 130 provides the liturgical language of hope. This is a powerful psalm. The setting of the psalm is ambiguous. Yet two things are clear. First, the psalmist is at a great distance from God. And, second, the speaker is painfully self-conscious of just how alienated he or she is from God. Thus there is a desperate quality to the opening petitions.

Structure. Psalm 130 separates into four parts. Verses 1-3 move quickly through a cry for help (vv. 1-2), a confession of sin (v. 2), and the realization of grace in God (v. 3). The remainder of the psalm moves out of the insight of v. 3 and begins to explore hope both for the psalmist and for the community of faith because God is gracious (vv. 4-8).

Significance. Psalm 130 is an excellent counterpart to Ezekiel 37, because it provides language of hope even for exiles. Psalm 130 reflects the setting of the exile. The opening cry for help in vv. 1-2 underscores how distant God is, while the confession of sin in v. 3 underscores how the consequences of sin go far beyond what any human action could do to improve the situation. These insights bring the psalmist to the ultimate truth that in the end only God can undo our alienation in a broken world—only God can forgive sin. This revelation is the turning point in the psalm, which provides the basis for the soliloquy on hope in vv. 5-8. The conclusion of the psalmist points us firmly toward Easter.

New Testament Texts

The texts are united by a concern to speak about life. The new life of believers in Christ is a major Lenten theme, and certainly on this fifth Sunday, with these passages before us, we must deal with "New Life in Christ."

The Epistle: *Romans 8:6-11*

In the Spirit and the Spirit in You

Setting. This passage is part of the larger section of chapters 5–8. As we recognized in considering earlier portions of this section of Romans, Paul's main focus here is on the way the Romans live with one another in the community of faith as they experience God's grace.

Structure. Actually 8:1-17 forms a thought unit on "life in the Spirit." Verses 1-2 are a kind of thesis statement, both summarizing earlier passages and pointing toward an overt statement about the Spirit. Verses 3-11 are a two-part elaboration on the thesis of vv. 1-2. First, vv. 3-8 explain the thesis, as is indicated by the opening word, "For. . . . " Second, vv. 9-11 juxtapose a remark to the statements in vv. 3-8 ("But . . . "). Finally, vv. 12-17 issue a series of conclusions ("So then . . . for . . . for . . . for . . . and if . . . ").

Significance. By starting the lesson at v. 6, one avoids the contrast between the inability of the law to achieve salvation versus God's achievement of salvation for humanity by sending the Son. Verse 6 provides a smooth start for this meditation, but there is a liability in taking vv. 6-8 out of their context. Independent of the definite setting provided by vv. 1-5, one is adrift without sail or rudder for sailing through the reflection on "flesh" and "Spirit." The danger will be to reduce the contrast to the level of the human versus the divine, or worse to contrast matter and spirit. As heirs to Greek thought, especially elements of Plato's dualism, which devalued the physical or real in deference to the spiritual or ideal, we may easily misunderstand Paul.

The apostle is not lapsing into a Platonic dualism here. Rather, he is using the antinomic language of apocalyptic eschatology to contrast spheres of power. *Flesh* for Paul can, and sometimes does, mean the real physical human self, but when set over against *Spirit* Paul employs the word metaphorically to designate powers other than and often in conflict with the power of God. Paul says to invest your confidence in any power other than God is to choose that which indeed is impotent. It is a bad investment, leading to bankruptcy rather than security; or, to use Paul's own language, death rather than life and peace. Looking anywhere other than to God for one's true security necessarily causes a separation from God, which means that one is at enmity with God. Paul's point: Don't put your trust in anything other than God. (One immediately wonders who would knowingly turn to anyone or anything other than God as a source of ultimate security? Answer: We all do, all the time! Paul does not address this problem here, but some attention to this topic in the course of preaching this text would be very helpful to a congregation that takes such matters for granted.)

In vv. 9-11 Paul's remarks become more positive in character. He declares who we, as believers, are: we are in the Spirit, and the Spirit is in us. This is the distinguishing mark of the Christian. Paul's turn here is deliberate. With all the previous admonition to set our minds on the Spirit rather than the flesh, we might easily but mistakenly conclude that our salvation is but a matter of making the right decisions. Wrong! We do have the responsibility to orient our lives toward God, but the good news of the gospel is that not only are we called to be in the context of the Spirit but that the gracious gift of God to us is that the Spirit dwells in us. Here is the mystery of salvation. We grasp for God because God has already grasped us. Indeed we are renewed internally as well as externally. The mind-boggling nature of the mystery of grace is seen in the comforting but confusing cluster of phrases Paul uses in vv. 9-11: "in the Spirit"; "the Spirit of God dwells in you"; "the Spirit of Christ"; "Christ is in you"; "the Spirit of him who raised Jesus from the dead dwells in you . . . his Spirit that dwells in you." It is finally impossible to make clear, rational sense of the collection of phrases, but what seems plain is that the division between humanity and the presence and power of God has been eliminated through God's work in Jesus Christ, especially as we know that work in the power of God, which raised Jesus from the grave. In the Resurrection of Jesus we perceive the presence and the power of God, which has now grasped us in order to bathe us in saving grace.

The Gospel: *John 11:1-45*

Jesus: The Resurrection and the Life

Setting. After the reading in John for last Sunday, Jesus gave a speech about his being the good shepherd and the door of the sheepfold; then, we heard of his going to Jerusalem for the Dedication festival where a controversy arose with the result that some sought to kill him while others believed. John 11:1-54 is the next major unit of the gospel—before the coming of the final Passover (11:55) which Jesus attended in Jerusalem.

Structure. The lesson—11:1-45 for the ambitious (or, perhaps more selectively, vv. 17-45 for those seeking more manageable material) is part of the larger passage, 11:1-54. The complete unit divides into seven scenes, several of which, for preaching, are capable of standing independently or being grouped. The seven scenes are (1) Jesus receives news of Lazarus's illness (vv. 1-5); (2) Jesus and his disciples (vv. 6-16); (3) Jesus and Martha (vv. 17-27); (4) Jesus and Mary (vv. 28-32); (5) Jesus at the tomb (vv. 33-41a); (6) Jesus raises Lazarus (vv. 41b-44); and (7) the council's thinking about Jesus (vv. 45-54). The full text for this Sunday covers the first six of the seven units and dips into the final one.

Significance. The whole chapter preserves, remembers, elaborates, and employs a story about the raising of Lazarus to make profound christological, especially soteriological, statements. In form, this story is another miracle with description (v. 1), healing (vv. 39, 44), and confirmation (vv. 44-46). But, the elaborated account bears an important message for the readers ("Jesus said to her, 'I am the resurrection and the life. Those who believe in me, even though they die, will live, and everyone who lives and who believes in me will never die. Do you believe this?' ").

Again, a quick march through the text provides numerous stimuli for preaching and writing the liturgy. Scene One: Here we learn of the basic problem, Lazarus's sickness. Four times in these five verses we are told explicitly of the illness. We learn that the illness occurs for "God's glory, so that the Son of God may be glorified through it." This odd statement raises an event in the human world to the level of particular divine purpose—the revelation of the glory of God.

Scene Two: In the conversation we find two themes—Jesus' journey to Jerusalem that leads to his death and his journey to Lazarus that leads to the raising of Lazarus from the dead. The two are inseparable. Jesus' behavior, waiting two days before going to do something about the problem, shows that his activity is determined by God's purposes in relation to the sickness and death. The report of the disciples' misunderstanding Jesus' metaphor about Lazarus's "falling asleep" allows Jesus to teach that faith is to be strengthened, not in relation to power, but in relation to Jesus himself.

Scene Three: When Jesus arrives, Martha is confident of his ability to help. His power, which she perceives, is the ability to intercede with God; it is not his person or an inherent capacity. Again, there is a misunderstanding. Jesus says Lazarus will rise, and Martha thinks of final resurrection. In turn, Jesus speaks explicitly with regard to the last days—a Christian's confidence of salvation is not merely for the future, but for the here and now. Jesus refers to himself as "the resurrection and the life." This is more than a pleonasm. Christian life begins now and continues despite death, because the Christian invests faith in Jesus himself.

Scene Four: Jesus' meeting with Mary is very different from the encounter with Martha, though the opening statements are the same ("Lord, if you had been here . . . "). Mary shows no overt confidence; thus there is no dialogue about resurrection and life with inherent revelatory, christological remarks. Jesus spoke earlier about himself and his power, but here we find no such declarations.

Scene Five: When Jesus sees the mourners, John tells us of his distress and anger (vv. 33, 38). The atmosphere of grief and mourning are characteristic of no faith. Jesus was also sorrowful. The Greek text contrasts the weeping of the crowd and the weeping of Jesus. The crowd "weeps and wails" (Greek = *klaiō*—a kind of formal funeral behavior); whereas Jesus "cries" (Greek = *dakryō*—a spontaneous bursting into tears)! Jesus' tears are certainly for the suffering of Lazarus, but they are also for the human situation of darkness, which leads to such faithless behavior. The crowd superficially recognizes Jesus' tears and reacts sympathetically, but with no understanding of who he is.

Scene Six: Jesus prays and gives a theological explanation for his activity. The bystanders hear Jesus and are thereby exhorted to faith. Then, the raising comes! The boldness of Jesus' voice and his command to the crowd demonstrates his power and majesty. Overtly the dead Lazarus is raised to life though the power of God working through Jesus.

Scene Seven: The snippet of this scene in our lesson simply declares that some believed—in contrast to the mention of hostility in the following verses.

In sum: Jesus is the source of life, "eternal life"—namely, an existence qualitatively and quantitatively greater than life without

Christ. This life is ours personally, but it always draws us into community and discipleship (see 13:34-35 and 15:1-17).

Lent 5: The Celebration

The emphasis as we prepare for Easter is on the Resurrection, which is ours in the power of the Spirit through the grace of Christ. We are like the dead multitude seen by the prophet; we are as dead as Lazarus in the tomb, reeking of corruption. We are given life by the power of the Word—the word of the prophet, the Word made flesh in Jesus Christ.

The preacher's great temptation will be to deal with either the valley of dry bones or the raising of Lazarus and to ignore the epistle altogether. It is important, however, to see the epistle as the hermeneutical link between the two extended narratives. The epistle will help keep a christological perspective on the Old Testament, and its emphasis on the Spirit will prevent an exposition of John from degenerating into a Jesu-centrism. To take either narrative in isolation and preach from it only in the language of ethical allegory (the unconverted are like dry bones; it takes preaching to revive the unconverted; and so on) is to shy away from the Paschal mystery, which should be at the heart of today's proclamation.

With such great texts, the preacher will need to limit carefully the content of the sermon. Today's lessons should be an adequate reply to those who say they never use the lectionary because after three years it is all used up! If it has been neglected, the practice learned in seminary of writing out the central message of the sermon as a control upon the content of the interpretation should be employed for this sermon.

Because of the length of the lessons, some abridgment may be in order, regrettable as that is in this era of sound bytes. The short form of the Gospel (vv. 17-45) might be used if the primary text and reference is from Ezekiel. If John is to be the primary text, then Ezekiel might be reduced to vv. 12-14 (as in the Roman rite) with a brief introduction to set it in context.

"THE GREAT REDEEMING WORK": PRAISE, PRAYER, AND PREACHING IN HOLY WEEK

This week, culminating in the celebration of the Resurrection, is at the heart of the Church's liturgical life, for it gives meaning to everything the Church does during the rest of the year. It is therefore important that the ordering of public worship and the preparation of sermons be done with a concern for "the basics," for retelling and remembering the story of salvation in such a dynamic fashion that the participants may become aware of their own involvement in God's story.

The posture of the worshiping Church is not that of those who are ignorant of how the story is going to turn out, or of the original disciples as they experienced the horror of the crucifixion and the fear of a similar fate. As Fred Pratt Green's hymn "To Mock Your Reign, O Dearest Lord" illustrates, we do not enter Holy Week ignorant of Easter Day, and that fact informs the character of our celebration. "Celebration" is still an appropriate word, even for the Good Friday liturgy, because the Church's celebration is always of God's triumph over sin and death, as a sixth-century hymn writer knew:

> Sing, my tongue, the glorious battle,
> sing the ending of the fray;
> now above the cross, the trophy,
> sound the loud triumphant lay;
> tell how Christ, the world's Redeemer,
> as a victim won the day. (UMH, 296)

Holy Week may be divided into three sections: (1) Passion or Palm Sunday; (2) Monday, Tuesday, and Wednesday; and (3) the Paschal

Triduum [three days] of Maundy Thursday, Good Friday, and Easter Day—which, in its turn, may have the vigil or night service and the service during the day. Because of space limitations, this year's volume will deal only with the lessons of Passion Sunday and the Easter Vigil. Good Friday's lessons will be in the Year B volume, and Maundy Thursday's in Year C. We will discuss the liturgies for all the days of the Triduum, however.

Perhaps the greatest surprise for many in the new structuring of the lectionary and calendar is the changed approach to Palm Sunday, which is now referred to as The Sunday of the Passion or as Passion/Palm Sunday, but not as Palm Sunday only. This means, of course, that the Fifth Sunday in Lent is no longer called Passion Sunday, as it was in the old calendar. It remains simply the Fifth Sunday in Lent. This change emphasizes the centrality of the Passion of Christ in the liturgical celebrations of Holy Week itself, and it prepares us more fully for the solemn observance of the Triduum. Palm Sunday, then, is not a kind of dry-run for Easter, and it is not intended to lay all the emphasis upon the triumphal entry in such a way as to allow those who only attend church on Sunday to miss the message of the cross. It is at least Passion/Palm Sunday, reminding us of the reason for the entry into Jerusalem.

Holy Week, by its very character as the time for specific remembering of the events of the Passion, stands out from the rest of Lent. This is accented visually by changing from the purple paraments or the Lenten array to a somber blood red color for paraments and vestments. Ideally these should be designed for this week in particular, rather than using the same red set as will appear at Pentecost. The red itself should be different in hue, darker than the brighter, red-orange of Pentecost.

The service for Passion/Palm Sunday is divided into two parts. The first is the Entrance Rite (the Liturgy of the Palms), which centers around the narrative of the entry into Jerusalem. This experience may begin out-of-doors or in the parish hall and then include a procession of all the people into the church for the second major part (the Liturgy of the Passion) which centers around the reading of the Passion narrative from controlling Gospel for the year. (The Passion according to John is always read on Good Friday.) There should be some obvious contrast between the "Hosannas" of the first part and the "Crucify!" of the second. The entry into the church should begin to mark a difference in emphasis as the people prepare to hear the Old Testament lesson. By the conclusion of the service, the congregation should be thinking seriously of what it means to spend the ensuing week in the shadow of the cross.

In the event of inclement weather or for some other reason the entire service needs to be done within the church itself, proper planning can still provide for a processional. The choir and minister should enter the chancel in silence and as unobtrusively as possible. When all are in place, the minister greets the people and offers an appropriate opening prayer. In Year A, Matthew 21:1-11 is read, and then there may be a blessing and distribution of the branches (if they have not been distributed at the door upon arrival). Notice that these should be branches that the participants can wave. Then, during the singing of such hymns as "All Glory, Laud, and Honor" and "Hosanna, Loud Hosanna," the choir leaves the chancel, processes through and around the nave, and returns to the chancel by way of the center aisle. It is appropriate for the people to file out of the pews and process around with the choir. This is liturgical dance at its most basic and most inclusive, because one does not need rhythm to participate!

Great care should be taken when preparing for any dramatic reading of the Passion narrative. Participants should be well rehearsed. Scripts are available that divide the Gospel into readers' parts. The preparation for this reading may well involve a special Lenten study group as the readers explore the Passion narrative in intensive Bible study. This may be a project for the confirmation class, particularly if its leadership can compensate for having the actual confirmations on this day, rather than waiting until the more temporally significant Eastertide.

The lessons for Monday, Tuesday, and Wednesday in Holy Week are the same all three years of the lectionary cycle. Their intent is not to review the events of the original Holy Week day by day, but to provide the faithful with a context within which to prepare to participate fully in the celebration of the mysteries of our salvation during the Triduum. The Old Testament lessons (Mon., Isaiah 42:1-9; Tue., Isaiah 49:1-7; Wed., Isaiah 50:4-9a) are from the first three servant songs and remind us of the servant character of the Messiah. The epistle lessons (Mon., Hebrews 9:11-15; Tue., I Corinthians 1:18-31; Wed., Hebrews 12:1-3) direct our thoughts to the themes of the cross and atonement. The Gospel readings (Mon., John 12:1-11; Tues., John 12:20-36; Wed., John 13:21-32) serve respectively to identify Jesus as God's anointed, whose death is part of a divine necessity that will result in the glorification of both God and Christ.

Maundy Thursday is referred to in the Revised Common Lectionary as "Holy Thursday," presumably following the new Roman Catholic usage. A strong case may be made for "Maundy," however, based on the concluding verse of the Gospel (John 13:1-17, 34): "a new commandment I give to you." "Maundy" derives from *mandatum*, the Latin word for "commandment." It is this new commandment that Jesus illustrates at the Last Supper by washing the disciples' feet, which congregations may observe on this day by the liturgical act of washing one another's feet.

The primary emphases of the day are the remembrance of the holy meal that Jesus celebrated with the disciples "on the night in which he was given up for us" (the Last Supper) and thanksgiving for the institution of that holy meal of remembrance through which he has been present with the Church through the ages (the Lord's Supper). The new Roman Catholic practice has been to emphasize the former since they have the Feast of Corpus Christi on which to do the latter. Protestant churches, particularly those which celebrate the Lord's Supper only occasionally, need to balance these emphases. White paraments rather than passion-red might be more appropriate for this service. Care should be taken not to give the impression of play-acting the Last Supper and thus identifying that meal as the only one that informs the meaning of the Lord's Supper. Even on Maundy Thursday this is still the bridal feast of the Lamb and is celebrated by a Church that has had the Emmaus experience. It is instructive that the gospel readings for this service do not include any of the synoptic accounts of the Last Supper. What we hear about the Last Supper is from Paul who identifies all later commemorations as eschatological proclamation. The gospel reading is from John, who does not describe the actual meal at all. Rather, his emphasis is on the washing of the disciples' feet, Jesus doing a kind of "show-and-tell" about the meaning of his ministry.

Planners of worship for Maundy Thursday need to keep in mind the balance between the historical event two thousand years ago and its identification with the Passover experience of Israel, and the present event in which Christ still makes himself available to his people and makes them a sacrament for the world. If the Washing of Feet is observed, it is natural to have it follow the reading of the Gospel and the sermon. Following that, the offertory hymn or anthem should be one of praise and thanksgiving for the gift of the Holy Communion. Hymns during Communion should also express joy for the sacrament, rather than anticipate Good Friday and the Crucifixion. It is after Communion that the aspect of the service changes and the people prepare to recall the suffering and death of Jesus.

Following the prayer after Communion, the following versicle and response might be used:

V: And when they had sung a hymn
R: **They went out to the Mount of Olives.**

Then, while the congregation sings a hymn such as " 'Tis Midnight, and on Olive's Brow," the altar and chancel are stripped of all decoration. The altar cross is veiled in dark red or black, and the people leave in silence.

The Good Friday service should be thought of as a continuation of the Maundy Thursday service. The people return in silence to the setting that they left the night before. The service begins in silence and proceeds quickly to the lessons and the reading of John's Passion narrative. This reading may also be done with members of the congregation taking the various parts, so that the congregation as a whole is the crowd. The sermon today is expected to deal with one or two of the major themes that emerge from the lessons. Additional liturgical resources for today can be found in *The Book of Common Prayer* and *Handbook of the Christian Year, Revised 1992.*

Passion Sunday

Old Testament Texts

The Old Testament texts are very appropriate for Passion Sunday. Isaiah 50:4-9*a* explores the call of the suffering servant, while Psalm 31:9-16 is a lament from the perspective of one who is suffering. As we will see, both of these texts share a similar three-part structure and probe the meaning of suffering from different perspectives.

The Lesson: *Isaiah 50:4-9a*

A Call to Discipleship

Setting. Isaiah 50:4-9*a* is the third of the suffering servant songs (Isaiah 42:1-4[5-9]; 49:1-6; 50:4-9*a*; 52:13–53:12). The first song was the lesson for Year A, Baptism of the Lord (see volume 1). You may want to refer to this lesson for a discussion of the individual and collective interpretations of these songs, since that discussion also applies to our present lesson. In the first servant song (Isaiah 42:1-4[5-9]), God is the primary speaker in declaring the choice of the servant. In the second song (Isaiah 49:1-6), the servant affirms his call already from the womb, but then doubts the purpose of it all with the claim that he has labored in vain. This song ends with the divine proclamation that the servant has not labored in vain but is called to be a light to the nations. The lesson for this Passion Sunday is an individual lament (or perhaps better an individual psalm of confidence) by the suffering servant. Here there is no longer any doubt about the purposefulness of being called. The servant is confident in being called to be God's pupil or disciple, no matter what circumstances may occur.

Structure. Isaiah 50:4-9*a* separates into three parts. In vv. 4-5*aa* the servant proclaims his call. This opening section is framed by the phrase, "The Lord GOD has given me the tongue . . . has opened my ear. . . . " Verses 5*ab*-6 describe the servant's training in discipleship. The song closes in vv. 7-9*a* with the suffering servant confessing the reliability of God's salvation. This closing unit is framed with the confession, "The Lord GOD helps me . . . "

Significance. The third suffering servant song presents a blueprint for discipleship, for it illustrates how theory and praxis must be one for any follower of God. The opening section of the song in vv. 4-5*aa* roots the authority of the servant in the call of God. In the opening and closing phrase, "The Lord God has . . . , " the servant makes it clear that he has been called to speak for God (the Lord has given him a tongue) and to hear the word of God (the Lord has opened his ear). The servant then tells us that his commissioning to hear God's word is for the purpose of discipleship. We are told in v. 4 that every morning God awakens the servant so that he is able to hear God's instruction like a pupil (Hebrew, *limmûdîm*; NRSV translation, "to listen as those who are taught"). The second section of the song is marked in v. 5*ab*, when the servant refers to himself and his present situation. In vv. 5*ab*-6 the servant outlines his training in discipleship. Here the work of God is translated into action. The servant does not rebel from God's instruction but accepts suffering in the present time. The final section (vv. 7-9*a*) shifts the focus back to God, and in so doing the servant provides the content of what he has learned as God's disciple, which now allows him to endure suffering. The content of God's tutoring is the proclamation of salvation which frames this unit in vv. 7 and 9 ("The Lord GOD helps me"). This confession allows for further affirmations about God's salvation by the servant in v. 7 and a direct address to his oppressors in v. 8. In v. 7 the two "therefores" state the servant's resolve to be a disciple, because God is near. In vv. 8-9*a* the servant addresses his opponents through a series of questions: "Who will contend with me?" "Who are my adversaries?" "Who will declare me guilty?" The answer, of course, is no one.

The striking thing about this suffering servant song, which must be emphasized in preaching, is how easily it moves between the images of student and suffering activist, between knowing the content of salvation in the classroom and doing the work of salvation. Neither theory nor praxis is allowed a special role over the other in the servant's soliloquy on discipleship. The servant is able to endure suffering because he knows that God is savior. Here doing is knowing and knowing is doing. This inseparable symbiosis goes to the heart of Passion Sunday.

The Response: *Psalm 31:9-16*

Living on God's Time

Setting. Psalm 31:9-16 builds on Isaiah 50:4-9a. It, too, is about suffering. It builds on Isaiah 50:4-9a because Psalm 31:9-16 explores the interior dimensions of the psalmist during the time of suffering in a way that the suffering servant song did not. Although the suffering of the servant in Isaiah 50:4-9a was intense, the point of view of the passage was on God and God's reliability during times of suffering. Because of this focus, we were never allowed to separate the servant's suffering from God's presence and salvation. Because of this, Isaiah 50:4-9a is probably best categorized as a song of confidence. Psalm 31:9-16 takes us further away from the security of God's salvation by exploring the experience of suffering itself. By taking us inside the experience of the suffering psalmist (especially in vv. 11-13), Psalm 31:9-16 becomes a true lament, where confessing the salvation of God is not enough. God must be called upon directly for salvation.

Structure. The psalm for this Sunday is only a fraction of Psalm 31. Most scholars would divide the psalm between vv. 1-8 and vv. 9-24. There is debate, however, on how these two parts are meant to interrelate. Each section appears to be an independent lament. Are they separate psalms that have been brought together? Are they parallel psalms that describe the same experience with increasing intensity? In addition to these larger questions of structure, we should note that a more natural break in the psalm would have been vv. 9-18, since vv. 19-24 are a song of praise that concludes the previous laments (vv. 1-8, 9-18). This discussion of the larger context of Psalm

31 suggests that vv. 9-16 can function well as a unit, even though the call for salvation actually extends through vv. 17-18. Psalm 31:9-16 can be separated into three parts: a call for salvation in vv. 9-10, a description of the psalmist's situation in vv. 11-13, and a confession in, along with a renewed call for, God's salvation in vv. 15-16.

Significance. The structure of Psalm 31:9-16 provides an interesting parallel to the suffering servant song of Isaiah 50:4-9*a*, because it separates into three parts that show roughly the same movement: from a focus on God, to the experience of the psalmist/suffering servant, and then back to God. However, as noted above, the movement of Psalm 31:9-16 takes us much more deeply into the experience of the psalmist, which makes this more of a lament than a song of confidence. Although God is the object of the psalm, and, indeed, looms large beneath the surface in every verse, it is the experience of the psalmist, who is presently at a great distance from God's salvation, that takes up most of the imagery. The opening call for salvation in vv. 9-10 (''Be gracious to me, O LORD'') gives way immediately to a physical description of the psalmist. Not only are her eyes dissolving (Hebrew, *'šš;* NRSV, wasted) from grief, but her very bones are also dissolving. Verses 11-13 move us from a physical to a social description of the psalmist. Here we learn that this person radiates dread (Hebrew, *ḥerpâ;* NRSV, the scorn of) to both friends and enemies (v. 11). She is the walking dead (v. 12). This is not idealized suffering. In fact there is no confidence here at all—nothing to grab on to because terror is on every side (v. 13). Up to this point, Psalm 31 has described the agony of social alienation and physical breakdown from personal threat. Yet, it is here that life itself is also clearly seen for what it is: We all live on God's time (v. 15). This revelation brings the psalmist outside of herself and back to God with a confession of trust, along with a renewed call for salvation in vv. 14-16. In reading this psalm and in identifying with the psalmist, we move through the dark pit and dread of Passion Sunday.

New Testament Texts

Both texts are concerned with the passion and death of Jesus. The brief liturgical piece in Philippians 2 speaks of the ''mind'' of Christ, indicating the selfless, sacrificial obedience that brought Christ to his death on the cross. Matthew offers no such summary, but rather the story of Jesus' final hours of suffering and death, though the telling of the story contains sufficient details and commentary from the evangelist to direct our reflection on Matthew's particular view of the Passion.

The Epistle: *Philippians 2:5-11*

Having the Mind of Christ

Setting. The Philippian congregation was the first European church founded by Paul, and it was one with which he maintained a very positive relationship. He was in prison at the time he penned this letter, and he seems to have written for several reasons: (1) to thank the Philippians for their support, physical and spiritual; (2) to discuss Epaphroditus's visit to him on behalf of the Philippians; and (3) to address difficulties and potential problems in the life of the church. Paul spends time early in the body of the letter exhorting the Philippians to unity, beginning at 1:27. In the course of that admonition, he holds Christ himself up in a formal fashion as the model and source of Christian harmony.

Structure. Since the late 1920s, innumerable scholars have studied Philippians 2:(5)6-11, attempting both to demonstrate that this portion of Philippians is a ''Christ-hymn'' from the life of the early Church and to determine the hymn's structure, origin, authorship, and theology. At the heart of debate about structure is whether the ''hymn'' is concerned with celebrating two movements (Christ's humble emptying into human form and Christ's exaltation to heavenly Lordship) or three states (preexistence/human life/resurrection-exaltation). While these issues are still studied and debated, interpreters are moving toward a middle-ground that recognizes the importance of all the elements of both schemes. Whatever the analysis, however, v. 5 is regarded as prose, leading up to the hymn; and vv. 6-11 are seen as the ''hymn'' per se.

Significance. Five major theological and christological statements are articulated: First, the remarks about Jesus Christ's being in the form of God are a metaphorical expression of the conviction of his preexistence. With notable exceptions, few interpreters read the line otherwise. The importance of this interpretation should not be missed. Here, in one of the earliest preserved documents of Christianity, is the confession of Christ's preexistence. Often historians assume that belief in preexistence came later in the development of Christian doctrine, but Philippians is evidence to the contrary. Equally remarkable is that Paul, the former Jew, includes and approves such a belief, for there is no evidence that Paul had abandoned Jewish monotheism to make this statement. Second, Christ's earthly existence is declared by using the metaphor of slavery. What does it mean to say that Christ took the form of a slave? The metaphor points to his humble obedience to the will of God and to his faithful service to his fellow human beings as he did God's will. Third, we hear of Christ's death. The mention of the cross in connection with the death points to the degree of humiliation Christ suffered to be faithful to God and humankind. His service was costly. He did not live to a ripe old-age and enjoy the fruits of his happy life of service. Indirectly Paul is telling the Philippians (and us) that the Lord died in order to be obedient and faithful—thus, what can disciples expect? Fourth, Christ's exaltation-resurrection is declared. The phrase, "therefore God also," introduces this element of the confession. Clearly Christ's being raised and his subsequent exalted status are God's work. Notice too that the language ("therefore") reaches back and relates God's action to Christ's own emptying and self-sacrifice. Fifth, we learn of Christ's cosmic rule. His self-giving unto death that issued in God's exalting him makes him the ruler of the cosmos. The phrases describing the "knees" indicates that all the denizens of heaven, earth, and hell will acknowledge Christ's rule. And the point of that rule is given with the words, "unto the glory of God the Father."

The Gospel: *Matthew 26:14–27:66*

"This is Jesus, the King of the Jews"

Setting. Matthew's presentation of the Passion is colored by his theological perspective. There are striking parallels between the development of the infancy narratives in Matthew 1–2 and the presentation of the scenes in the Passion narrative. Matthew opened with Herod, the chief priests, and the scribes conferring to destroy the baby Jesus and ended with Pilate, the chief priests, and the scribes conspiring to eliminate Jesus. As the Gentile Magi were positively inclined toward the baby Jesus, so the Gentile wife of Pilate is on his side during the Passion. Moreover, the characters in the Passion story—disciples, women, Pharisees, chief priests, and scribes—were active throughout the earlier portions of the Gospel, so that consideration of their roles in the Passion is clarified by viewing their broader action in the Gospel.

Structure. The Passion can be broken into large or narrow compartments. In either case, we should not lose sight of the essential unity of this portion of Matthew's story of Jesus. Let us consider the broad structure of the narrative: preliminary events are told in 26:14-29 (the plot between Judas and the chief priests, and the Passover with the institution of the Lord's Supper); 26:30-56 focuses on the prayer and the arrest in Gethsemane; 26:57–27:10 recounts the events related to the Sanhedrin's trial, including Peter's denial and Judas' suicide; 27:11-31 narrates the Roman trial, the decision to crucify Jesus, and the mockery by the soldiers; and 27:32-66 tells of the Crucifixion, death, and burial. All of this material precedes the Matthean resurrection stories in chapter 28.

Significance. In essence, Matthew follows Mark's account of the Passion (assuming the priority of Mark). Matthew handles Mark critically but conservatively, merely clarifying Mark's storytelling (compare the details of Jesus' comings and goings in Gethsemane, Matthew 26:36-46 and Mark 13:32-42). But Matthew alters the narrative to give it his own emphases by adding certain materials. Seven items merit comment:

First, *Jesus* is not merely a name in Matthew's Passion. It is also a title. In Matthew 1:21, the reader learned that Jesus was he who saves his people from their sins. Indeed, the Greek *Iēsous* translates the Hebrew *yešuah*—meaning help or salvation! In contrast to Mark, Matthew opens major sections of the Passion narrative with the name-title *Jesus*. We repeatedly encounter the phrase *now Jesus*. . . . Furthermore, the sign over the cross reads, "This is Jesus, the King of the Jews,'' but in Mark it says, ''King of the Jews.'' Matthew tells the story of Jesus—the story of God's help or salvation.

Second, the image of Jesus is heightened throughout this account. His foreknowledge of events is stressed (see 26:25). And at the arrest, he is clearly in charge of the events: He addresses Judas authoritatively and directly; he scolds the disciples; he speaks of his own power; and he reveals his dedication to fulfillment of the will of God.

Third, we are given additional material about Judas. We see him defile the Temple by throwing back the ''blood-money,'' so that he leaves the Jerusalem Temple authorities ''holding the bag.'' In this way, Matthew ''points the finger'' concerning the guilt for Jesus' death.

Fourth, we have in Matthew's account the story of Pilate's wife. This part of the narrative heightens the claim of Jesus' righteousness. Like Joseph in the Infancy narrative, she is a ''dreamer,'' receiving divine communications, but she is a Gentile and so foreshadows the day when the gospel will be universally available to Jew and Gentile alike without prejudice.

Fifth, Pilate washes his hands—clearly a symbolic disclaimer of guilt with a symbolic transfer of responsibility.

Sixth, Matthew seems harshly inclined toward the Jews at this point in the narrative. His story points to the depravity of Israel. But, as recent scholarship increasingly insists, this is a pointed momentary statement not to be interpreted either out of its context in Matthew or without awareness of the strong Matthean polemic against the Jewish leaders of his own time. This is not a timeless damnation of the Jews, much less prophecy. We must ponder Matthew's account of Jewish behavior with extreme caution. Past preaching has often launched into anti-Jewish harangues with shameful and disastrous results. Matthew's point is that Jesus came offering salvation, but salvation was rejected. The Jews of this narrative are but typical of humanity's pattern of relating to God throughout history. We look God in the face, and not liking what we see, we reject God.

Seventh, at 27:9 we read for the last time in Matthew's Gospel that prophecy was fulfilled. The story continues, however, in fulfillment of the promises Jesus himself made.

In sum: Matthew portrays Jesus as the lordly master of his own fate. He goes to the cross in fulfillment of prophecy and, thereby, achieves God's will ("all righteousness"). When we see Jesus' suffering and death, we see salvation—costly, compassionate, and gracious. But with prophecy now fulfilled, we wait for what lies ahead!

Lent 6 (Passion Sunday): The Celebration

For suggestions about the Passion Sunday liturgy, see the previous commentary on Holy Week.

The hymn "All Praise to Thee, for Thou, O King Divine" is a paraphrase of today's epistle, so where there is a concern about the length of the service, it may serve as a hymn or anthem connecting the Old Testament lesson to the reading of the Passion.

It may be overwhelming for the preacher to decide how to preach or what to preach about on this day when faced with such a marvelous array of scripture from which to choose. If the reading of the Passion narrative has been well done, the preacher may feel it anticlimactic to say anything at all! The sermon should be focused and to the point, rather than attempt to deal with every aspect of the Passion story in one presentation. One approach is to use the epistle as the hermeneutical key to presenting the theology of the Passion according to which gospel narrative is read.

Although the primary emphasis of the day is on the Passion rather than the triumphal entry, it might be helpful in congregations where this liturgical approach is new to help them see how the entry is a part of the Passion sequence and how it introduces us to what is to follow throughout Holy Week. Matthew, for example, wants his readers to see the connection of the entry to the prophecy of Zechariah. The significance of the prophecy and its fulfillment for Matthew may lie in the description of the king as the meek or gentle one. It is the same word as in the Sermon on the Mount, "Blessed are the meek, [*praeis*]" and in the saying which only Matthew preserves, "Learn from me, for I am gentle." Of the four evangelists, only Matthew uses the word in his gospel. This gentleness is compatible with upsetting the tables of the money-changers, for it is a gentleness that comes from single-minded devotion and a willingness to rely on God rather than on one's own power and intelligence. This is the ''mind of Christ'' of which Paul speaks in the epistle, the gentleness of Christ to which he refers in I Cor. 10:1. There may be times when we experience God's dealings with us as violent, but for most people, most of the time, the quality of God's way is gentle. In the Passion, it is the gentle God who suffers violence.

Holy Week begins with the choice of a donkey and a foal, to remind us of the way that God deals with us. It is the way of George Herbert's prayer, ''Gentleness'':

> Throw away thy rod,
> Throw away thy wrath:
> O my God,
> Take the gentle path.

EASTER: CREATION'S EIGHTH DAY

Although Easter is the central, formative event in the Christian revelation and although it is the day of the largest attendance of the faithful at church, it frequently has an anticlimactic character after all of the emphasis put into Lent. Easter Day, the day toward which the Lenten solemnity has been directed, ends up marking both the high point in the year's attendance and the beginning of the downward spiral toward the summer low point.

Perhaps Easter is finally mystery, a wonderfully overwhelming mystery, and the human creature cannot bear for long what it cannot understand. We are familiar with the miracle of birth, and so we concur with the sentiment that Christmas should be kept all year long. I have seen men and women leave the church weeping after the solemn stripping of the altar on Maundy Thursday, because we know what it is to have rejoicing turned into mourning, to surrender the brightness of life to the shadow of death. Maybe that is why Easter is so unbearable: it dares to proclaim a reality opposed to what we experience in the natural realm. We hear no one suggesting that we keep Easter all year long, even though the observance of the Lord's Day every seven days intends precisely that!

The new calendar and lectionary seek to make us aware that Easter is more than one day in the year and to restore the historic observance of the Great Fifty Days, the time from Easter Sunday through the Day of Pentecost. No longer do we speak of Sundays ''after Easter'' but ''of Easter,'' reminding us that the celebration is an ongoing event in the Church's life of prayer and proclamation. Pentecost is not the first day of a new season; it is the last day of the Easter festival, uniting the events of the Resurrection and the empowerment of the Church. The Great Fifty Days are observed as a unit because they are presented that way in the Lukan chronology. In John's Gospel, the risen Lord breathes the Holy Spirit upon the apostles on the evening of Easter Day. The Christian year achieves a kind of liturgical harmonization of the Gospels by placing the Day of Pentecost in the evening of the season. The observance of sacred time thus helps teach us that the Resurrection, the Ascension, and the gift of the Spirit are mutually dependent events participating in the same theological reality. Each presupposes the others.

It has been known in the history of Christian preaching for the Easter proclamation to lose its radical character and for the theological center to be ignored in the interest of making the day more palatable to modern sensibilities. This began early in the English-speaking world, because the day was called "Easter," after the pagan goddess of spring, rather than some form of *Pasch*, which was the practice in the Romance languages. The pagan symbolism has frequently dominated the observance and turned it into a kind of vernal rite, complete with the fertility images of eggs and rabbits. Spring symbolism has become the content of the Easter message, and resurrection is reduced to a biological necessity, a regeneration of the earth, while we rejoice in our hymns that "Flowers make glee among the hills,/And set the meadows dancing"! It is salutary for those of us in the northern hemisphere to remember that in half the world Easter occurs in the autumn.

The radical proclamation of Easter has also often been compromised through substituting a Platonic doctrine of the immortality of the soul for the biblical concept of resurrection. Eternal life is seen as something we have a "right" to rather than the free gift of God in Jesus Christ. To the degree that we are immortal, it is in relation to what God has done in salvation rather than creation. This salvation is the cause for our Easter proclamation and celebration.

As Lent has dealt with the issue of mortality, beginning with Ash Wednesday, so now Easter celebrates that immortality which is God's gift, the antidote to sin's poison. The Easter Vigil has been restored in the practice of many churches because it presents, in a unified fashion, the story of sin and salvation in the lessons and applies that through baptism to the life of the individual believer, who is made a part of the Body of Christ and is nourished spiritually at the Lord's

Table. Pastors and worship committees unfamiliar with the Vigil should consult *The Handbook of the Christian Year, Revised 1992* to find a copy of the service and helpful commentary about it.

Many preachers and worship leaders are dismayed when they first look at the list of lessons for the Vigil and the length of the service. It is at this point that they need to remember that the liturgy was made for them and not they for the liturgy. Without endorsing some kind of liturgical minimalism, it is possible to ask what is reasonable for a congregation unfamiliar with this particular tradition and what is most important within this service.

Historically, the Vigil was the time for the baptism of those who had received instruction and for their participation for the first time in the Lord's Supper. The reading of the history of salvation lasted through the night, leading to the baptism, the illumination, of the converts as the sun began to rise and they were buried and raised with Christ in baptism. This intricate interweaving of story and song, light and darkness, water and oil, touching and being touched, and bread and wine is eloquent testimony to the Church's understanding of the liturgy as a multimedia event!

For churches locked into an hour time-frame, it is obvious that the Vigil in its fullness will have difficulty gaining acceptance. Pastors 0might wish to think of spreading the components of the Vigil out over a period of time. This maintains the sequence of events in their integrity, and as the individual parts are observed during the earlier Sundays of Easter, they help the congregation focus on the Paschal mystery throughout the season.

The four sections of the Vigil (Light, Word, Water, Eucharist) may be divided among the first three Sundays of Easter by doing the service of light as part of the traditional sunrise service, the service of the Word as the "regular service" on Easter Day, the administration of baptism on the Second Sunday of Easter where the epistle reading from I Peter will be appropriate, and the Lord's Supper on the Third Sunday of Easter when the gospel reading is the Emmaus narrative. The Fourth through the Seventh Sundays of Easter may then be devoted to what has been called "mystagogical catechesis," training in the meaning of these sacred mysteries in which we have participated.

This volume deals only with the texts of the Vigil and not with the service on Easter Day, because the texts of the Vigil are central to understanding the celebration, and they can appropriately be transferred to the later service. The readings for the later service are the same for each of the three years of the cycle and will be included in the Year B edition.

Baptism is central to our celebration of Easter, and Easter is central to our understanding of baptism. The Lord's Day is the eighth day of creation, the day of the new creation brought into being by Christ's victory over death. In a time when baptism is the center of so much theological discussion and controversy, pastors and laypeople might do well to explore and experience the meaning of baptism from a liturgical perspective rather than argue about its meaning in terms of arid rational categories.

This may mean "saving up" baptisms for Easter, so that there will be individuals ready to receive the Easter sacrament. This in itself testifies to an understanding of baptism that mantains that it is not an individualistic rite but a community one. The baptisms might be spread across the Great Fifty Days. This allows some convenience in timing, but it also emphasizes the meaning of the whole season. More than one baptism should be done at a time whenever possible, however, so as not to lose the communal nature of the event.

The renewal of baptismal vows is a part of many Vigil services, especially if there are no baptisms to be administered. If there is no Vigil, as with other components mentioned above, the renewal may find an independent place during one of the other Sunday services of the season. The major service of Easter Day itself is preferable, since the renewal service can be a vivid reminder of what brings everyone, the regulars and the one-timers, together in the Christian family. A brief form of baptismal renewal may be used for the rest of the Sundays of Easter at the beginning of the service as part of the entrance rite and in place of the confession of sin, as follows:

> Alleluia! Christ is risen.
>> The Lord is risen indeed. **Alleluia!**
> Let us pray.
> God of the Covenants,
> we thank you for this gift of water
> which gives fruitfulness to the fields

and refreshment and cleansing to your creatures.
Water witnessed to your goodness
when you led your people through the sea
and satisfied their thirst from flinty rock.
You consecrated your Son
in the waters of the Jordan,
and through water
you have given us a new birth from above.
May this water remind us of our baptism,
and let us share the joy
of all who have been baptized this Easter.
We ask this in the name of the Risen Christ.
                                                    Amen.
Sprinkling water towards the people, the minister says:
Remember your baptism and be thankful.
The service continues with the opening hymn.*

Baptisms are possibly the most ecumenically segregated events in the Christian Church. The sign act that is understood to incorporate us into the catholic Church is most often observed in congregational isolation. Easter can be a time to realize the fullness of the sign by administering baptism in conjunction with other congregations, so that its ecumenical character is realized. This can easily be done when two or more churches celebrate the Easter Vigil together.

*Based on a prayer for the blessing of water in *With All God's People: The New Ecumenical Prayer Cycle—Orders of Service,* John Carden, ed. (Geneva: World Council of Churches, 1989), p. 110.

Easter Vigil

Old Testament Texts

The Old Testament lessons for the Easter Vigil represent a wide sweep of texts that explore the mighty acts of God as both savior and creator. The central text for the Easter Vigil is the account of Israel's salvation at the Reed Sea in Exodus 14:10-31; 15:20-21. The actions of God in our world—from creation to the full realization of a distant future salvation—are all viewed in light of the reality of Israel's salvation at the sea. This event will also be our lens as we read through the lessons for the Easter Vigil service.

The Text: *Genesis 1:1–2:4a and Psalm 136:1-9, 23-26; Genesis 7:1-5, 11-18; 8:6-18; 9:8-13 and Psalm 46; Genesis 22 and Psalm 16; Exodus 14:10-31; 15:20-21 and Exodus 15:1b-6, 11-13, 17-18; Isaiah 55:1-11 and Isaiah 12:2-6; Baruch 3:9-15, 32–4:4 and Psalm 19; Ezekiel 36:24-28 and Psalms 42–43; Ezekiel 37:1-14 and Psalm 143; Zephaniah 3:14-20 and Psalms 98 and 114*

Salvation History

Setting. There are nine Old Testament lessons for the Easter Vigil, and each has a hymnic response. They include: creation (Genesis 1:1-2:4a; Psalm 136:1-9, 23-26); God's covenant with the earth after the flood (Genesis 7:1-5, 11-18; 8:6-18; 9:8-13; Psalm 46); the obedience of Abraham in being willing to sacrifice Isaac (Genesis 22; Psalm 16); salvation at the Reed Sea (Exodus 14:10-31; 15:20-21; Exodus 15:1*b*-6, 11-13, 17-18); a reaffirmation of God's covenant promise to exiled Israel (Isaiah 55:1-11; Isaiah 12:2-6); a call for Israel to learn God's wisdom (Baruch 3:9-15, 32–4:4; Psalm 19); a future vision of a new land (Ezekiel 36:24-28; Psalms 42–43); a future vision of a new people (Ezekiel 37:1-14; Psalm 143); and, finally, a future vision of Zion (Zephaniah 3:14-20; Psalm 98). These passages present an account of the history of salvation. They review the past mighty acts of God from creation and provide us with glimpses of how God intends to carry salvation through to its conclusion of a new Zion. Our review of these passages will not include the hymnic responses.

Structure. Exodus 14 is the central text in the Easter Vigil because the recounting of the history of salvation in the Old Testament always begins with the experience of salvation. It is only out of Israel's experience of God's salvation that they are able to look backward and see the hand of God in creation and in their very formation as a people (Genesis lessons) or to look forward and confess with confidence future acts of God's salvation (the prophetic lessons). Thus Exodus 14 is the prism that brings God's past and future acts of salvation into focus, and as such we should view it as the central text in the larger structure of lessons.

Significance. The event at the Reed Sea is singled out as the central event of salvation in Exodus 14:10-31; 15:20-21. The Reed Sea event focuses us on Israel's passing through the water and God's victory over Pharaoh and his army. This passing through the water has traditionally encouraged an interpretation of salvation as being a transformation from death to life or from slavery to freedom. Although the text is certainly about a transformation that signals Israel's salvation, the poles in the transformation are not as absolute as life versus death or slavery versus freedom. Such absolute contrasts require that we pit Egypt against life in the promised land of Canaan, and Exodus 14 does not give us that. Instead Israel's experience of salvation is a transformation from Egypt to the wilderness, from being slaves of Pharaoh to becoming slaves of God. This new form of slavery is life, which inaugurates a journey in the wilderness, where

Israel follows God. In the wilderness Israel is able to look back and see the hand of God in its formation, and it is able to look ahead with hope to the day when it would finally reach the promised land. These two perspectives provide the structure and significance to the lessons of the Easter Vigil.

The three lessons from Genesis fill out Israel's past. The first two lessons provide insight into God that is not evident from the experience of salvation itself. Genesis 1 underscores that the savior is indeed also the creator, thus God's salvation at the Reed Sea is very secure. Genesis 7–9 shows how God is obligated to bring about a new creation that is free of sin. God's obligation is explored through the theme of covenant in Genesis 9. The final lesson in Genesis shifts the focus from God to Abraham. Genesis 22 illustrates the important role that the people of God play in God's commitment to bring about a new world by idealizing the faith of Abraham.

The (primarily) prophetic lessons sketch out God's future salvation for Israel, the nations, and the entire creation. Isaiah 55:1-11 returns to the theme of covenant to proclaim confidently that God's word will inevitably accomplish its goal, and that because of this the people of God have a mission. Baruch 3:9-15, 32–4:4 is a call for wisdom both to see the hand of God in the present/future and to walk in God's ways. Ezekiel 36:24-28 and 37:1-14 explore the distant horizons by describing how God will indeed bring the people to the land and thus breathe new life into the people. Both of these visions, however, are meant to function as encouragement for Israel to walk in God's ways in the present. Finally, Zephaniah 3:14-20 goes beyond the immediate horizon and provides the outline of a future Zion when God's commitment to a new creation will reach its goal. This future (eschatological) vision brings us around again to Genesis 1 (a pristine creation where evil is in check), so that in many ways the Old Testament lessons for the Easter Vigil present a large circle.

The Old Testament lessons for the Easter Vigil underscore how salvation, as a crossing through the water, puts us on a journey with God in the wilderness. The stark landscape allows us to see the hand of God in our past, which in turn provides the content for our future hopes. God must bring about this future, and we must simply remain faithful travelers. Psalm 114 underscores the central focus of the Exodus for celebrating God's salvation. This text may be used as a concluding summary to the Easter Vigil.

New Testament Texts

Both texts are concerned with declaring the significance of the death and Resurrection of Jesus Christ for his followers. Romans focuses primarily on the death of Christ, but speaks of the altered reality of life that comes through being alive in Christ Jesus. Matthew tells of the tomb and the appearance of Jesus to the women, not overtly commenting on the death, but presupposing it.

The Epistle: *Romans 6:3-11*

Dead, Buried, and Alive in Christ Jesus

Setting. In considering portions of chapter 5 we have already recognized that Romans 5–8 forms a large unit concerned with the life of the Christian community as it experiences grace. Within these four chapters of Romans, there are sub-units. Romans 6:1–7:6 forms one section of the larger whole, explaining how those who are justified live differently from the way that they lived prior to God's gracious right-wising of them. Furthermore, within 6:1–7:6 there are three clear phases of Paul's argument. Our text, 6:3-11, occurs within the first movement of Paul's reasoning, which comprises 6:1-14, a statement about a Christian's transformation from death to life.

Structure. Paul forms his argument from an assumption, namely that those reading the letter are themselves baptized. The chronology of Jesus' experience—death, burial, Resurrection—sets the markers for Paul's teaching about what it means for Christians to be "in Christ." There is constant motion back and forth between focusing on the Christians and focusing on Christ: we/Christ/we/Christ/we/Christ. Ultimately in verse 11 Paul turns directly to the Romans, but even here he recognizes a thorough identification between the Romans and

Christ, "So you also must consider yourselves dead to sin and alive to God in Christ Jesus."

Significance. This passage informs us, directly and indirectly, of several things. Indirectly, we can read between the lines to see that early Christians thought and taught about baptism in relation to Jesus' death (and perhaps burial); and they understood that through the death of Jesus a gain was achieved and that the benefits of Christ's death were transferred to the believers—either actually or symbolically in baptism. Paul assumes such thinking in mounting his argument to the Romans. He also assumes the Romans will comprehend his statements that build off the idea that Jesus Christ is a representative figure. Earlier (5:12-21) Paul treated Adam and Christ as universal representatives of humanity, speaking in apocalyptic categories about the "first" and "last Adam." Similarly, in Romans 3:21-25 Paul cast Jesus as a universal human, taking up the language of the Jewish sacrificial cult to say that Christ died "for all who believe." In that same vein, here, Paul applies the death, burial, and Resurrection of Christ to the lives of the Roman Christians. Paul explains what it means to be "in Christ" by stating that what happened to Christ has also happened to believers.

Paul contemplates the past, the present, and the future of the Romans "in Christ." In their pasts, they died with Christ to sin. Paul understands that sin is a cosmic power—he even personifies it in his argument in Romans to dramatize its role in opposition to God. Effectively, sin deceived humanity and took humankind captive. Under the sway of the power of sin, humans were in bondage. Only when they died could humans escape sin's grasp. Christ himself freed humanity from sin by dying as a universal figure, so that through his death a benefit was won and, in turn, imparted to all who are now (as Paul would put it, by grace through faith) "in him." Also in the past, the Romans were symbolically buried with Christ in their baptism; and in the future, they will inherit the benefit of Christ's Resurrection as they will themselves be raised from the dead. All of this has profound meaning for the present. Believers are now freed from sin, because they died with Christ to sin. And as they look to the future in hope of resurrection, they are freed from sin and free for the living of a new life, which itself is a prolepsis of the resurrection life to come.

The mind-set behind this argument and its basic logic will seem strange to moderns whose imaginations have been dwarfed by a post-enlightenment scientific worldview. This passage articulates the mentality of a poet. How can we communicate such a message today? At the roots of Paul's statements are these theological themes: grace, hope, and freedom. In approaching this powerful but difficult text, we must remember that Paul is not evangelizing the Romans. He is standing alongside them and (1) calling up their past and (2) reminding them of their future, in order (3) to speak to them about the quality of their lives in the present. Grace, hope, and freedom are respectively the themes of these times. In preaching we may need to develop a temporal scheme similar to Paul's and, then, talk of the times using metaphors and images appropriate to the particular theological theme of each time.

The Gospel: *Matthew 28:1-10*

He Is Not Here

Setting. After the Passion narrative, Matthew tells a series of stories about the Resurrection of Jesus. Some of these go beyond Mark's final episode of the empty tomb, so that Matthew, when compared with Mark, differs both subtly (by telling the tomb story in his own way) and obviously (by offering additional material) from Mark. At the time of his writing, Matthew's community was invloved in missions, and these stories point to the foundation of their work.

Structure. These verses can be seen as one large story, but even so, there are two distinct scenes linked together by a narrative bridge. First, we learn of the events at the tomb (28:1-7); then, the women leave to tell the disciples (28:8); and finally Jesus appears and speaks to them along the way (28:9-10).

Significance. The nuance that Matthew brings to his account of the Passion narrative is seen in the subtle way in which he modifies the telling of the story in comparison to Mark's version of the events. Clearly, Matthew heightens the divine elements of the narrative. Mark had a young man at the tomb, and from the clothing mentioned (''a white robe'') one immediately thinks that the young man is an angelic figure. Matthew makes the identity of this figure plain—he is an angel descended from heaven, and his appearance is startling and brilliant. Moreover, we are no longer left wondering how the stone was moved from the mouth of the tomb (as we were in Mark); for, in Matthew, the angel moves the stone. Furthermore, Matthew refers to happenings that make the awesome nature of this scene quite clear (as if the physical appearance of the angel would not inspire awe), telling of the earthquake that occurred when the angel descended (the second such rumbling—see 27:51) and of the utter terror of the guards at the tomb (themselves a new element of the story). God never appears in the story, but God is clearly the director of all this action.

Matthew also overtly improves the performance of the women in his telling of the story. They do not merely leave in fear, even if that means reverential fear of the Lord! They leave, and we are told that they intend to tell the disciples what they have seen and heard, as they were directed to do. The fear they feel is mixed with and overcome by joy, so that their fear is clearly the fear of the Lord.

But beyond these somewhat obvious changes, we have in 28:9-10 the account of the appearance of the risen Jesus to the women. This report is remarkable, for the risen Jesus has absolutely nothing new to say beyond what the women have already heard from the angel at the tomb. Moreover, we know that they intend to tell the disciples what the angel instructed them to communicate, so that Jesus' appearance is neither necessary in order to provide additional information nor required to ensure correct execution of their commission.

So what difference does this appearance make? Perhaps it means nothing more, and nothing less, than that the risen Jesus is present as his followers go about the faithful performance of their divine commissions. This interpretation of the story is consistent with the "Emmanuel-theology"—namely, the strong conviction that Christ is "God with us," which characterizes the beginning and the ending of the First Gospel.

In Matthew's telling of this portion of the story of Jesus' Resurrection, we see clearly that the raising of Jesus is the work of God, that the good news of Jesus' Resurrection empowers his followers to share the message of God's work through him, and that in their faithful execution of their commissions, believers are not alone but in the presence of the risen Lord Jesus Christ. The theology of this story is clearly oriented toward declaring the strong hand of God at work in the Resurrection of Jesus Christ. The story assumes and focuses on what God is doing in and through Jesus Christ, and it is a message of comfort and hope for those of us who read it with eyes to see.

How do we preach this passage? Perhaps we turn to the moods generated among the characters in the account. The angel is majestic and causes awe. The guards fall back in genuine fear. The women are faithful and obedient. And above all, Jesus is present. There are a variety of ways in which the preacher can correlate, illustrate, and declare these elements of Matthew's Resurrection narrative.

Easter Eve or Day: The Celebration

The lessons and liturgy today point to an event for proclamation rather than explanation. We have here good news to be shared rather than analyzed. This good news can have a positive effect on the interaction between preacher and laypeople. The lessons and liturgy, for example, have been emphasizing water imagery and its use as a sign of salvation. We remember the Passover and are reminded that we have been buried with Christ in baptism.

The preacher may construct the sermon on different grounds if we remember that these are baptized folk who are being addressed. Congregations may be pleased to discover that the preacher addresses them as brothers and sisters in the faith rather than as objects of an incessant missionary enterprise!

The following two stanzas from Charles Wesley fit well as a response to the reading of today's gospel from Matthew. Or the last stanza may serve as a dismissal after the benediction. The text calls for a strong Long Meter tune such as Truro or Duke Street.

> Haste, then, ye souls that first believe,
> Who dare the gospel word receive,
> Your faith with joyful hearts confess,
> Be bold, be Jesus' witnesses.

Go, tell the followers of your Lord
Their Jesus is to life restored;
He lives, that they his life may find;
He lives to quicken humankind.*

Because the Apostles' Creed is the historic baptismal creed, its use during all the Sundays of Easter is appropriate as another remembrance of baptism.

*J. Allan Kay, ed., *Wesley's Prayers and Praises* (London: Epworth, 1958), p. 112.

Second Sunday of Easter

Texts from Acts and Psalms

In the weeks of Easter, readings from Acts replace the normal Old Testament lessons. Several of the Acts readings are closely related to one another. Thus, in the sections on "Setting" and "Structure" for the text from Acts, information is given that is relevant for this Sunday's reading from Acts, as well as the next two Sundays. The material will be given only in this chapter. Readers will be reminded in the subsequent two weeks to refer back to this information. A portion of the Psalm for this week is actually quoted in the course of Peter's speech.

The Lesson: *Acts 2:14a, 22-32*

Jesus: Attested, Rejected, Raised, and Proclaimed

Setting. Acts 2 is a neatly structured and practically self-contained unit. Verses 1-13 locate the early Christian community in time and place, and recount the miracle of Pentecost. These lines give a portrait of the cosmopolitan crowd present at Pentecost and tell of the divine anointing of the disciples with the Holy Spirit; furthermore, we learn of the crowd's misunderstanding of the disciples' behavior. The story is peculiar, for sometimes we have an outbreak of glossolalia, sometimes a miracle of speech in unstudied languages, and sometimes a miracle of hearing in one's own tongue words spoken in another language. Whatever the original form or forms of this story, Luke offers an account of the spread of the gospel as the result of an eschatological (miraculous) act of God.

115

Verses 14-40 are the speech by Peter (with some interaction with the crowd) on Pentecost. Verse 41 rounds off the speech scene by providing a conclusion; and vv. 42-47 summarize the situation among the believers in Jerusalem in the earliest days.

The lessons from Acts 2 do not include verses 14*b*-21, but it is impossible to understand the mood and tone of the parts of Peter's speech (vv. 22-32 and 36-41) and the subsequent report about the community's life (vv. 42-47) without viewing these parts of Acts 2 in relation to vv. 14*b*-21. In these verses, Peter addresses the misunderstanding of the masses. He explains not only that they are wrong in believing the disciples to be drunk but also that the events they are witnessing are to be understood in relation to the prophecy of Joel concerning God's outpouring of the Spirit on humanity in the last days. Indeed, God works in this manner in the last days so that "everyone who calls on the name of the Lord shall be saved" (v. 21). Thus Pentecost is a splendid eschatological event!

Structure. Verses 14-16 focus on the situation. In v. 14, Peter speaks, addressing the misunderstanding directly. The texts from Acts 2 for the Second and Third Sundays of Easter both begin with the report of Peter's move to address the crowd. Then, the bulk of our lesson for this week (vv. 22-32) is the second major movement of the speech, which actually runs from v. 22 through v. 36. This section presents christological teaching in vv. 22-24. Then, vv. 25-36 offer scriptural proofs and accompanying arguments to authenticate the Christology.

Significance. With the time identified in eschatological terms of judgment, vv. 22-24 deliver christological kerygma. Peter's claim is that God acted through Jesus. Peter maintains that the divine plan is fulfilled in and through Jesus. Notice that though the death of Jesus fulfills the plan of God, it does not exculpate humans who moved against Jesus. The form and tone of these lines, with their densely cast relative clauses, is that of early Christian confessional material: "Jesus of Nazareth, a man attested to you by God with deeds of power, wonders, and signs that God did through him among you, as you yourselves know—this man, handed over to you according to the definite plan and foreknowledge of God, you crucified and killed by the hands of those outside the law. But God raised him up. . . . ''

Having given the christological teaching, or made the christological claims, Luke has Peter give scriptural proof of the christological kerygma in vv. 25-36. The basic scriptural proof comes from Psalm 16, but Psalms 110 and 132 also bolster the christological arguments. This is not exactly ''prooftexting''; rather, in a common manner of ancient argumentation, scriptural evidence is offered as precedent for the teaching given. Beyond the formal boundaries of the lesson, v. 33 makes an explicit connection between the Christology and the events at hand on Pentecost.

For preaching one may do well to focus on the christological claims of the text rather than attempt to recover the faded dynamics of the arguments from scripture. The logic of the associations between the Christology and the Psalm texts would be an excellent topic for church school teaching, but it would most likely cause confusion (or boredom) in a sermon.

There is a linear quality to this speech: (1) Jesus was attested by God. (2) Jesus was rejected by humans. (3) But God raised Jesus, showing God's power, God's plan, and God's presence. (4) To all this, Christians are witnesses. This linear logic may guide the sermon, but the last item may provide the goal for the proclamation of this passage. Beyond merely rearticulating the rich christological textures of this text (make a list of the titles and references to Jesus!), one can move to challenge the congregation to take seriously their role as witnesses of the work of God for the salvation of humanity in Jesus Christ. We might ask ourselves how well we could manage the situation that Peter and the disciples faced that day—with the general public looking at us, misunderstanding us, assuming embarrassing (though false) things about us because of the effects of our faith. What would we do? Would we poke our heads in a hole like an ostrich and pretend or hope the whole thing will go away? Or, would we seize the moment for Christ and use the attention to declare the gospel? Perhaps our call is not merely to reenact the activities of the disciples on that first Pentecost, because their world is not ours; but we are called to show the same devotion and courage as ''witnesses.''

The Response: *Psalm 16*

Full Confidence in God

Setting. This Psalm is usually designated a psalm of trust. It is similar to Psalms 4, 11, and 21. The character of such psalms is the reverent utterance of tranquil assurance that God is the fountainhead of life's greatest delight. Generally such psalms lay out the reasons for praising God, occasionally after making an appeal for divine aid (as in this psalm). Scholars conclude this psalm was composed in the post-exilic period because of (1) the close parallels (perhaps even literary relationship) between v. 4 and Isaiah 57:5-6; 65:4, (2) the presence of Aramaisms in vv. 5-6, and (3) the "wisdom" style of language and logic.

Structure. The Psalm falls naturally into three parts, vv. 1-4, vv. 5-8, and vv. 9-11. The opening verses explore the idea that apart from God there is no good to be found. The remainder of the text first declares the psalmist's sense of security by speaking of the good heritage that comes as we choose the Lord as the holder of our lot, and then declares the psalmist's gladness and confidence that God will not "give [us] up to Sheol."

Significance. This psalm is a natural partner for the reading from Acts 2, because in the course of the Pentecost sermon, Luke has Peter quote this very text. Acts 2:25-28 is a reiteration of the Septuagint version of Psalm 16:8-11. In Acts 2, the psalm has an explicit christological function, since it is related to Christ's own security and to his not having been given to "Hades" and "corruption."

Independent of the christological use of the text in Acts, this psalm elaborates on why God is the source of our full confidence, both for the present and the future life—earthly and hereafter. In focusing on earthly life, the psalmist declares that God is the God of both good times and bad times. Verse 6 states that God is present when things are going well for us, and then immediately v. 7 recognizes that God is present when the going gets tough. Moreover, because God is ever present, especially in hard times, we are secure. Verse 8 makes it clear that the psalmist is not talking about a "God of the gaps"—the kind of God we call in to get us out of a jam. God is "always before" us. God is to be one who sets the priorities of our lives. And because that is the case, we can, in all circumstances, "rest secure."

At heart, this psalm is a deep expression of reverent appreciation and devotion to God. One is sorely tempted to extract an admonition from the text—trust God fully whatever the circumstances. But the mood and purpose of the Psalm refutes such use of the text. The "should" in relation to this text is this: In worship we should let this Psalm function as a vehicle for our own praise of the good and dependable God to whom Jesus Christ and we give ourselves without reservation.

New Testament Texts

The New Testament texts for this Second Sunday of Easter explore the meaning of faith for post-Easter Christians. I Peter 1:3-9 probes the important role of faith in the larger context of Christ's work of salvation, where faith is both God's gift to us and our response to God. John 20:19-31 is a story that outlines the changing nature of faith when future disciples will no longer be able to see the risen Lord.

The Epistle: *I Peter 1:3-9*

Faith as Gift and Responsibility

Setting. All of the epistle lessons throughout this season of Easter are from I Peter. First Peter can be separated into four sections: a salutation (1:1-2), a baptismal discourse (1:3–4:11), a letter (4:12–5:11), and a closing (5:12-14). This outline underscores how the book separates into two main sections—the baptismal discourse and the letter proper. These two parts of the book contrast sharply in style, even though the theme of suffering is central throughout. The baptismal discourse outlines the nature and significance of Christian life in a balanced and solemn style and within this structure addresses issues of suffering, in contrast to the more direct address of the letter, where suffering appears to be more immediate in the life of the community.

The epistle lesson for this Sunday (vv. 3-9) is part of a grand opening statement (vv. 3-12) about the character of the Christian community in the light of the salvific work of God through Jesus. As we will see, faith is an important ingredient to this community.

Structure. The text can be divided between a call for the community to praise God for the gift of being "born again" in vv. 3-5, and a reflection on the meaning of being born again for the life of the community in vv. 6-9. The text can be outlined in the following manner:

    I. What it means to be "born again" (vv. 3-5)
      A. Hope
      B. Inheritance
      C. Salvation
    II. Genuine Faith as a Result of Suffering (vv. 6-9)
      A. Love
      B. Belief
      C. Salvation

Significance. The outline suggests a symmetry between salvation (vv. 3-5) and discipleship (vv. 6-9), with faith providing the link between the two. The central theme when preaching this text, therefore, is faith.

The content of God's salvation is described in three parts, which are marked in the Greek text with the preposition *eis* (to). By the mercy of God, the writer tells us, we are born again to (*eis*) a hope (v. 3), an inheritance (vv. 4-5a), and finally salvation (v. 5b). Each of these three aspects of being born again requires comment. First, hope: The writer tells us that the content of hope is life (it is a living hope), which was inaugurated with Jesus' Resurrection from the dead. Second, inheritance: Even though Jesus inaugurated hope by defeating death, he is not the object of hope. The object of hope is the inheritance of a new and undefiled world that was made through Jesus' Resurrection. In the context of this inheritance, faith enters into the text as part of the content of God's salvation. Although this inheritance is presently in heaven, the power of God generates belief in the lives of Christians, and this belief guards and preserves them for participation in this new realm here and now, even though its full realization must await a future time. Third, salvation: Salvation is the realization of the Christian's inheritance into this world. The three-part process of being born again is perhaps best summarized spatially. It begins with the resurrected Jesus in this world, moves to a new vision of creation in heaven, and returns to this world in the end time. Faith is an integral part of the content of God's salvation, for it links Christians here and now to the sphere of God's salvation, even though our inheritance is presently in heaven. Seen from this perspective, faith is less an activity of humans and more a gift from God. Thus it is part of the very content of salvation itself. Faith is a heavenly gift from God.

Faith, God's heavenly gift, is dynamic. Thus it is not simply something that Christians possess. Rather, it empowers us for action. The second part of the passage outlines the content of faith from the perspective of Christian activity in this world. First Peter 1:6-9 states that faith comes into clearest focus through suffering, for it is in such situations of suffering that all the alloys of faith melt away, and this prompts three activities in relation to Jesus: (1) Even though the risen Lord is not seen, the Christian loves him and (2) believes in him. (3) This combination of loving and believing in the unseen risen Lord will bring faith to its conclusion, which is our very salvation. Faith, as the activity of Christians in loving and believing in Jesus, pulls the heavenly inheritance of salvation into this world, which, in turn, makes our very salvation concrete. Faith is both gift and responsibility.

The Gospel: *John 20:19-31*

A New Type of Faith

Setting. John 20:19-31 is an account of the appearance of Jesus, first to the disciples and then to Thomas. Scholars classify this story as a post-Resurrection narrative. These types of stories usually include the following elements: the disciples are in a situation where they are mourning the loss of Jesus, then Jesus appears to them, greets them, the disciples recognize Jesus, which results in a word of command from Jesus to the disciples. The author of John uses the structure of the post-Resurrection narrative to explore faith.

Structure. The larger context of John 20 includes two other accounts of disciples encountering the risen Lord, which aid in developing the theme of post-Resurrection faith. First, the Beloved Disciple is presented as believing immediately without ever seeing the risen Lord (v. 8). Second, Mary Magdalene is presented as seeing the risen Lord but not recognizing him until Jesus speaks her name (vv. 11-18). Verses 19-31 present two more accounts of faith in disciples who encounter the risen Lord. Verses 19-23 are an account of Jesus' appearance to the disciples in the locked room, vv. 24-29 narrate the skepticism of Thomas, and vv. 30-31 outline a new type of faith. The text can be outlined in the following manner:

I. The Appearance to the Disciples: Seeing and Believing (vv. 19-23)
   A. Appearance at a Time of Mourning and Fear (v. 19)
   B. Recognition of Jesus (v. 20)
   C. Post-Resurrection Command (vv. 21-23)
II. The Appearance to Thomas: Seeing Is Believing (vv. 24-29)
   A. Doubt: Seeing Is Believing (vv. 24-25)
   B. Faith: Seeing and Believing (vv. 26-28)
   C. A New Kind of Faith: Hearing and Believing (v. 29)
III. The Rise of the Gospel and a New Kind of Faith (vv. 30-31)

Significance. The transition—from seeing the risen Jesus and believing in him (the disciples and Thomas) to hearing the good news of the gospel and believing in the risen Jesus (those referred to by Jesus in v. 29 and those addressed by the writer in vv. 30-31)—is the point of the passage. This transition requires a new understanding of faith, which the character of Thomas is meant to illustrate for us.

The appearance of Jesus to the disciples follows the expected form of post-Resurrection narratives. Faith in this situation can be described as "seeing and believing." These stories of the resurrected Jesus and his disciples always move to a command that incorporates a mission. In our text, the command of Jesus to his disciples is three-fold: a mission to the nations (v. 21), the gift of the Holy Spirit (v. 22), and the power to forgive sins (v. 23). There is a transfer here in the power of the resurrected Lord from Jesus to disciples. This transfer, however, requires a new definition of faith, for it implies the *absence of Jesus*. In the development of the story, Thomas represents this transition where "seeing and believing" can no longer be the content of faith. Thomas was not present to see Jesus, so the disciples must tell him about the appearance of Jesus, and in so doing, they are fulfilling the command of Jesus in vv. 21-23. Thomas is a negative example, because hearing is not enough for him; he, too, must see Jesus. By refusing to let go of this criterion, he turns the faith of the disciples (seeing and believing) into doubt (seeing is believing). His doubt is answered by another appearance of Jesus, but the point of Jesus' appearance is made clear in v. 29, when Jesus blesses those (future) disciples who will accept the message of the first generation of disciples and thus redefine their faith as "hearing and believing."

The evangelist enters the narrative in vv. 30-31 to provide even more content to the blessing of Jesus in v. 29. Here we learn that the Gospel of John is the content of what must be heard for us (those future disciples of Jesus) to have faith. Thus this Gospel is offered to us as the content of faith, which we are invited to act upon. Again faith is both gift and responsibility.

The power of this text is that it underscores how preaching is faith. The scripture lessons are faith as God's heavenly gift, and the preaching of them is the minister's action that pulls salvation into this world. Yet, that is not enough, for the only way that God's gift of faith can be let loose in our world is through the more extended activity of Christians beyond the worship service itself. Thus when preaching on these texts, the minister must not only proclaim that faith is God's gift but that it also includes a call for discipleship.

Easter 2: The Celebration

The substitution of lessons from Acts for the Old Testament lessons during Eastertide is not some Marcionite perversion of the liturgy; rather, it is an attempt to illustrate through the liturgy that the Church sees itself in the history of covenant that began in Genesis and continues through the witness of the prophets and apostles. Acts is reserved almost entirely for Eastertide to demonstrate that the New Testament Church was the result of the Easter event and was not a break with the past but rather a continuation of what God had been doing from the beginning. The intimate connection between Easter and Pentecost is emphasized by the use of Peter's speech in Acts 2 for the earlier Sundays of the season.

It is customary to read the story of Thomas from the perspective of one who doubts in the Resurrection. There may be some value in thinking of it as the story of one who is tempted to deny the Incarnation. The Gospel of John begins with its great hymn about the Incarnation; it now ends with this story of Thomas whose great fear may not be that Jesus lives forevermore but that he was never really human to begin with! Thomas is a warning to all those who would "spiritualize" the gospel out of the realm of the vulnerable and the material into a gossamer world of idealistic abstractions. Jesus may pass through doors, but he carries his wounds with him.

In many denominations the Second Sunday of Easter will be observed as COCU (Church of Christ Uniting) Sunday. This can provide an opportunity to affirm baptismal unity concretely and demonstrably among local churches across denominational lines in a way that relates to the Paschal mystery rather than merely to a program emphasis.

Third Sunday of Easter

Texts from Acts and Psalms

In bringing these readings together, the lectionary focuses our attention on making our vows to the Lord in the presence of all his people. The psalm meditates on fulfilling such a vow as an act of thanksgiving for all God's bountiful provisions for us, and the account from Acts shows us certain penitent persons at Pentecost publicly professing repentance and being baptized in the name of Jesus Christ in reaction to Peter's proclamation, "God has made him both Lord and Christ, this Jesus whom you crucified."

The Lesson: *Acts 2:14a, 36-41*

The Full Experience of Salvation

Setting. The reader can consult the section on "Setting" of last week's lesson for full information about the context of this passage from Acts 2. For this week's lesson it is helpful to notice the setting of the events narrated here in terms of the mood of the crowd. The people in Jerusalem on Pentecost are portrayed as less than impressed with the band of early believers. Indeed, the public estimation of the disciples is low: they are taken for a bunch of drunks. Imagine the attitude of the crowd at Pentecost as Peter arose to speak—they would be skeptical, scrutinizing, even ready to have a good laugh at the expense of one who had had a few too many. And then Peter speaks. The initial part of the speech registers the eschatological character of the time, and the following parts of the speech drive home the conflict between God and the crowd concerning Jesus. The attitude of the assembly is dramatically altered by the address.

Structure. Verse 14*a* presents Peter and positions him to speak and us (as readers) to hear. The shape of the lectionary causes v. 36 to become Peter's message. Then, vv. 37-40 rehearse an abbreviated form of the exchange between the crowd and the apostles, especially Peter. Verse 41 summarizes the outcome of the events.

Significance. The gospel message, as summarized in v. 36, has two distinct dimensions—one positive, the other negative. First, the gospel presents the good news that God has established Jesus as both Christ and Lord. This means that Jesus is God's chosen one, God's anointed one, set forth to be savior or redeemer of a humanity in distress. That Jesus is Lord means that God's work in Jesus transcends the encumbrances of time and space, giving him universal power to accomplish the crucial work for which God has set him apart. Second, the gospel delivers the bad news that humanity rejects God's work, particularly the one whom God designates as the divine agent for the achievement of salvation. God acts, and we react, spurning God's will; but God prevails. This message does not let us off the hook. We do not hear simply, ''You're okay!'' or ''God loves you, so learn to love yourselves.'' The gospel, as Peter preached it on Pentecost, confronts us squarely with our guilt—we stand in opposition to God; we even work actively against God. In the face of our guilt, however, the gospel declares that God is greater than we are; and we learn that God has the final say, despite our resistance.

In this way, the gospel simultaneously registers our guilt and gives us the source of our hope. As v. 37 says, ''Now when they heard this, they were cut to the heart and said . . . 'What should we do?' '' Neither the crowd at Pentecost nor we are shown our guilt merely to depress us; rather, we are called to acknowledge our failures so that we will eagerly turn toward God. Guilt, shame, and remorse are not cures in themselves; at best they are the beginning of an essential transformation of our selves in relation to God. In short, conviction (to be theologically valid) must lead to conversion!

The crisis of the crowd's conviction finds its solution in the track laid down in Peter's reply to their question, ''What should we do?'' He calls for the people to repent, to be baptized in the name of Jesus Christ, to experience the forgiveness of their sins, and to receive the Holy Spirit. In the case of the Pentecost crowd, the repentance called for is specifically related to their rejection of Jesus. In other speeches in Acts, when the people addressed by apostolic preachers had not in fact rejected Jesus, the call to repentance is more an appeal to believe the good news and to rearrange the priorities of life than it is a call to acknowledge guilt. Thus the history of the crowd determines the full meaning of repentance; though for all who repent, repentance is the complete reorientation of life toward God. Negatively, repentance can have different connotations; but, positively, repentance means that we live under the Lordship of Jesus Christ.

It is important to see the unity of the track of salvation that Peter declares. Repentance, baptism, forgiveness, and reception of the Spirit hang together! No single item in this list is separable from the others. Moreover, the elements are not strictly sequential, so that the doing of one will not guarantee the following of another. If this line were an automatic series of events, we could force forgiveness and the Spirit by doing repentance and baptism. Then salvation would rest with us rather than with God, who in Jesus Christ overcomes our resistance to save us despite ourselves!

The Response: *Psalm 116:1-4, 12-19*

Declaring Our Gratitude to God

Setting. From the initial verse in this psalm we learn that this psalm is an individual's declaration of gratitude to God for having delivered the psalmist from dire, nearly fatal, illness. The psalmist had not passively and pleasantly borne the illness, as is clear from the mention of "consternation" and the reported outburst, "Everyone is a liar!" in v. 11. This makes the joyous tone of the psalmist's thanksgiving all the more prominent.

Structure. The Septuagint divides this psalm into two psalms (Psalm 114 = vv. 1-9 and Psalm 115 = vv. 10-19), perhaps because there are two distinguishable parts to the whole: distress/deliverance and faith/vow. Verses 1-4 report the psalmist's distress; vv. 5-9 tell of the Lord's deliverance; vv. 10-14 declare the psalmist's faith and

127

report the vow; and vv. 15-19 state the psalmist's devotion to the Lord and reiterate the vow.

Significance. Reading the words of this lesson may remind some of us of Kris Kristofferson's song, "Why Me Lord?" Perhaps Kristofferson had read this psalm. It is a brief, but profound, expression of thanksgiving. Normally such a psalm would have been uttered in the Temple as the psalmist (or another person using the psalm) actually gave the thanks-offering that had been vowed during the sickness. The psalm narrates the realization of the vow, and it is itself a prominent element of the fulfillment of the pledge!

What does this psalm say to us? It reminds us that we give all too little thanks to God for the many good experiences in life. Our prayers are regularly filled with grovelling confession, pious babbling, and frantic petition (at best of an intercessory kind). This psalm shows us another way. The psalmist assumes a form of piety intent upon public display of real gratitude that is not immodest and that gives testimony to the goodness of God. The recognition of God's goodness and the discipline of expressing thanksgiving impart to the psalmist a true sense of identity: "I am your servant, the son of your serving girl." Thanksgiving has become an attitude, which gives a joyous outlook on life. The psalmist's thanksgiving is no mere duty; it is true pleasure and it becomes true testimony.

The thanksgiving described in this psalm is the positive side of the energy of a life oriented toward God. The call to repentance in Acts gave us a look at the negative side of faith—facing up to our failures. But, this text shows us the other side of devotion—facing up to God's successes. Expressing thanks for God's goodness helps us to recognize that God cares for us. This means that we are not merely worthy of our own scorn; rather we are creatures whom God deems worthy of his love. Thanksgiving helps us celebrate the goodness of God, and it gives us the eyes of faith to see ourselves and others as God sees us.

New Testament Texts

The New Testament texts explore a tension that is inevitable to post-Easter Christians. The tension concerns the fact that in Christ we are new people, who must enter the new world that the Resurrection of Jesus has inaugurated, even while we still live in this world. First Peter 1:(14-16) 17-23 describes this tension as being a sojourn in exile, while Luke 24:13-35 conveys the tension through the blindness of two disciples to the presence of the risen Lord walking with them on the road to Emmaus. The two lessons underscore how being Christian means that we have a foot in each of two different worlds.

The Epistle: *1 Peter 1:(14-16) 17-23*

The Implications of Being Holy

Setting. The baptismal sermon first examined last week continues in the lesson from I Peter for this week. Although the lectionary lesson begins in v. 17 with a call to fearful obedience during a time of exile, this unit should probably be read with the preceding three verses (vv. 14-16), which present a call for holiness, since the reality of God's holiness provides the basis both for obedience and the imagery of exile in vv. 17-23.

The primary meaning of holiness is separation. When we confess God to be holy, we are confessing that God is not part of the everyday activity of our world. Our mundane activity is profane in contrast to God, who is sacred. Thus central to the notion of holiness is separateness of God from our world, and some writers use the term *otherness,* or *The Holy Other* to describe the sacred character of God. The otherness of God is built into the very fabric of creation. Notice how the seventh day in Genesis 1 is holy and thus separated from the other six. Holiness, as indicating the separateness of God from creation, is developed further when the Fall of creation is introduced. Not only is the gulf between the sacred and the profane widened with fallen humanity and the cursed creation, but in addition, the presence of God in our world actually becomes a dangerous thing. Biblical writers frequently use the imagery of fire to convey this danger. For example, Moses must be warned about the imminent danger of God when he confronts the burning bush in Exodus 3, and this is also true of Israel at Mount Sinai in Exodus 19. Holiness (as separation) introduces a number of tensions for the people of God. One tension concerns salvation itself: Even though holiness is dangerous to us, we need it to be remade into the people of God. We must pass through the fire, for it both consumes and refines, judges and saves. A second tension concerns the life of faith: Once we have been remade by God, we too become holy, with the result that we are no longer part of this world even though we live in it. Thus the result of salvation is that we become sojourners and exiles in this world. First Peter 1:(14-16) 17-23 addresses both of these tensions.

Structure. The text can be outlined in the following manner:

I. A Call to Holiness (vv. 14-16)
II. The Tension of Becoming Holy (vv. 17-21)
    A. Fear
    B. Sojourning in Exile
    C. Faith
III. The Activity of Holiness: Love (vv. 22-23)

Significance. When explaining the call to holiness in vv. 14-16, the author of I Peter quotes the often repeated phrase from priestly legislation in the Pentateuch (Exodus 25–31, 35–40, Leviticus, Numbers 1–10), "You shall be holy for I am holy." Here the identity of the people of God is rooted directly in God's character. The consequence of being consumed and refined in conformity with God's character is that the people of God, too, become separate. Notice how the call to holiness carries with it a contrast between past passions and former ignorance and their present situation.

Second, the tension of holiness in vv. 17-21 is evoked through three motifs that are interrelated in this section. First, fear: One result of God's sanctifying action on us is fear. Fear is the proper response to the dangerous presence of God, for it indicates our awareness of salvation—namely, that we have been pulled into a world that is larger than our mundane routine, if not at odds with it. The story of Moses at the burning bush illustrates this point. Upon first appearance, Moses is only curious about the bush, though he should be frightened. This problem in the story must be resolved. Thus God must break into the story and comment on the dangerous character of the bush, after which Moses responds properly with fear. Second, separateness: Another result of God's sanctifying action is that we are made new and thus, like God, become separate from this world even though we still live in it. The tension of holiness is that we have a foot in each of two worlds and must continually remind ourselves that, as the sanctified people of God, life in the profane world has become a sojourn in exile. Third, faith: Faith is the Christian's link to holiness; it is our pipeline to God, which gives us identity and keeps the tension of holiness ever present.

Third, the activity of holiness is described in vv. 22-23. The author of 1 Peter could not be more clear at this point: To be consumed and refined in conformity with God's character frees us to love.

This text could easily be preached by itself. It confronts the contemporary Church with an aspect of God's character that we do not stress very often. In the last two or three decades (at least since the 1960s), we have successfully pulled God out of the sanctuary and heightened our responsibility for social action. As necessary and as good as our social action is (indeed the activity of holiness is love), this text reminds us that God is far more than ethics. God is holy and separate and thus dangerous to us and to this world. First Peter underscores that salvation is a far more radical thing than anything we can do for ourselves, which is why worship is essential for the Church. It is where we come to understand the holiness of God, and like Moses, learn what it means to be required to take our shoes off. The gospel lesson will explore the importance of worship in relation to God's holiness.

The Gospel: *Luke 24:13-35*

Being Blinded by the Familiar

Setting. The story of the two disciples on the road to Emmaus is perhaps the best known post-Resurrection narrative. Two disciples are ''on the road,'' they are journeying. This is a motif that has been central to Luke's construction of the life of Jesus, for his ministry on earth was also presented as a journey that culminated in his Passion in Jerusalem. In Luke 24:13-35 the Passion of Jesus is over, and now his journey is extended to these disciples. However, they are unaware of this extension, and they do not recognize that Jesus is walking with them. Through the motif of blindness in the two disciples, Luke addresses a problem that is presupposed in I Peter, but not addressed directly—namely, if God is holy and separate from us (which indeed the risen Lord is), where do we go to see Christ and thus become holy ourselves? And what are the obstacles? Luke 24:13-35 is a story about word and sacrament.

Structure. Luke 24 narrates the Resurrection of Jesus and his appearance to the women (vv. 1-11), to the two disciples on the road to Emmaus (vv. 13-35), and to the rest of the disciples (vv. 36-49), before it concludes with an account of Jesus' Ascension into heaven (vv. 50-53). The appearance of Jesus to the women provides an important context for the Emmaus story because it ends by noting how the disciples lacked faith in the message of the women and judged their report of a resurrection as being nonsense (NRSV, v. 11, "idle tale").

The two disciples on the road to Emmaus share the judgment of the larger group. Their story can be separated into four parts: an initial meeting with Jesus on the road (vv. 13-16), a conversation with Jesus (vv. 17-27), a meal (vv. 28-32), and their return to Jerusalem (vv. 33-35).

Significance. Clearly the story presents a transition from blindness to sight, from faithlessness to faith, and in the process, it presents a journey that ends where it began—in Jerusalem, with one significant difference: What was judged as nonsense in v. 11 gives way to a meal with the resurrected Jesus in vv. 44-49. The central task in preaching this text is to convey what events in the Emmaus story have allowed for this transition—namely, scripture and the Eucharist.

First, the context for Jesus' teaching scripture in vv. 25-27 is important to the narrative. The two disciples are absorbed in the events of Jesus' Passion. They know all the details of the events, and they even know all the rumors. In other words, they are familiar with all aspects of Jesus' story, but they are blind. Jesus, on the other hand, is presented as hopelessly naive. His questions even prompt one of the disciples to blurt out in v. 18: "Are you the only stranger in Jerusalem who does not know the things that have taken place there in these days?" Yet in the evolution of the story, the disciples are the fools, and they must be taught by Jesus.

Second, Luke also introduces eucharistic language into the story. Jesus takes bread, blesses, and breaks it, which provides the moment for the disciples to recognize the risen Lord. Recognition of Jesus in the Eucharist then allows the disciples to understand the previous teaching from scripture.

Where do we go to see Christ and become holy? In the Emmaus story, word and sacrament work in tandem to instill faith: "The Lord has risen indeed!" (v. 34). And what are the obstacles? In our familiarity with the Jesus story, we can lose the holiness that is central to it and in the process become blinded to the risen Lord. When this happens, Jesus becomes no more than an ideal of what we would like God to be and to do for us. We can reduce God to ethical behavior, which might not be linked to God's holiness.

Easter 3: The Celebration

The gospel lesson for today provides the preacher with the opportunity to preach about the Lord's Supper apart from the context of the Last Supper. There is value in preaching about the Lord's Supper on Sundays other than when it is celebrated, if only to address those who might seek to avoid those Sundays!

The popular mind still tends to think of the Lord's Supper generally in terms of the Last Supper. It is forgotten that the Last Supper only provides one facet of meaning to the eucharistic meal. Today, in the midst of Easter, we are reminded that the Lord's Supper is also a resurrection meal, one in which we anticipate the heavenly banquet. Charles Wesley called it the antepast of heaven, the same word as antepasto, what one eats before the main course comes along! Thus, we emphatically know that the Lord's Supper is a participation in the whole ministry of Jesus—past, present, and future. That is why the acclamation of the people in the midst of the Great Thanksgiving is "Christ has died; Christ is risen; Christ will come again."

One of Wesley's hymns is particularly appropriate for this day, because it is based on the Emmaus story:

> O Thou who this mysterious bread
> Didst in Emmaus break,
> Return, herewith our souls to feed,
> And to thy followers speak.
>
> Unseal the volume of thy grace,
> Apply the gospel word;
> Open our eyes to see thy face,
> Our hearts to know the Lord.
>
> Of thee communing still, we mourn
> Till thou the veil remove;
> Talk with us, and our hearts shall burn
> With flames of fervent love.
>
> Enkindle now the heavenly zeal,
> And make thy mercy known,
> And give our pardoned souls to feel
> That God and love are one. (*UMH* No. 613)

The first two stanzas may be used separately after the reading of the gospel and just before the sermon.

Although the title line of another hymn, "Abide With Me," is taken from today's gospel, the actual text of the hymn does not make it particularly appropriate for this day.

Fourth Sunday of Easter

Texts from Acts and Psalms

In the lesson from Acts, we are told of the early Christians' generosity toward one another and of the steady work of God in the life and growth of the Church. Psalm 23 celebrates God's securing care and bountiful provision for humanity.

The Lesson: *Acts 2:42-47*

Life in "the Last Days"

Setting. Again, readers should turn to the materials for the second Sunday of Easter for a discussion of the setting of this lesson in the context of Acts 2. In brief, vv. 42-47 summarize the situation in Jerusalem in the earliest days after the conversion of multitudes of people at (and following) Pentecost. The image of the social setting is clearly eschatological in nature. The conviction that they were living in "the last days" led these believers to a radically altered life-style. They are pictured as being continually in worship. They pooled their resources. And we read that "many wonders and signs were being done by the apostles."

Structure. These verses present a brief, straightforward summary of the circumstances among the Jerusalem believers. In rapid succession, we learn of these things: (1) devotion to a life of faith, (2) awe over signs and wonders, (3) generosity with regard to material possessions, (4) worship in the Temple, (5) fellowship and praise at table, and (6) growth of the community.

Significance. More than any other verses in Acts, these lines preserve the memory of the exhilaration of the believers in Jerusalem as they lived in the charged atmosphere of eschatological expectation, which permeated the life of the Church. Luke presents us with an idealized moment in early Christian history, focusing on all that was good among those first disciples. These verses portray the "golden era" of the life of the Church. Alas, as the story continues we learn that this moment was far too brief. Soon the apostles will be jailed for their preaching; soon Ananias and Sapphira will seek glory; soon the Hebrew-Christians and the Hellenist-Christians will be in conflict with one another; and soon Stephen will be murdered. But before all that happens the book of Acts tells us of this one moment in time when all was well.

Unfortunately things have never been so good again, or at least it seems that way. But lest we join the many others before us who have longed to return to this time and have sought to recreate the Jerusalem context by adopting the patterns of community life mentioned in these verses, we should remind ourselves bluntly that those first Jerusalem disciples sowed the seeds of their own demise by doing some of the striking things that we read about in this text. We refer especially to the pooling of resources, which turned out to be a shortsighted measure that ultimately exhausted their wherewithal and left them destitute and in need of a handout from congregations in other regions.

Nevertheless, while we may not want simply to return to the past to experience its glory and to repeat its mistakes, we can learn much about life in the Christian community during the best of times. Notice that the life of faith was the passion of all the people remembered here. Indeed, faith focused the life of these people with one another, so that they gave themselves to what they had in common, not what distinguished them from one another. In this context, the members of the community accomplished great things that, in turn, brought a sense of awe to the whole community. In part because they believed the end was at hand, but in part because they were living freely, beyond the level of sheer self-interest, these early believers could be extraordinarily generous. Seeing the goodness of God expressed in concrete terms in the life of the community freed these people to put others ahead of themselves, so that they became truly Christlike in selfless and sacrificial giving. This attitude of gratitude and atmosphere of generosity fostered a deep community-wide piety that culminated in worship and fellowship, which momentarily set them in good stead with the people of Jerusalem. And that goodwill eventuated in the growth of the community.

One could preach on the elements of a vital Christian Church by reflecting on the dynamics of the early Jerusalem community. We should not try to distill a formula for success from this account, as if we have been called merely to relive the past. But we certainly can learn something about the activities and attitudes of believers in the best of times. The sermon should avoid both nostalgia and chiding contemporary congregations for being something less than the Jerusalem church. The positive mood of this text should direct the sermon toward a positive goal, perhaps calling us in hope to give fully of ourselves and our blessings as a body of believers in Christ.

The Response: *Psalm 23*

The Security of the Divine Shepherd

Setting. The psalm is titled "A Psalm of David," and the pastoral imagery of vv. 1-4 remind us of King David as a shepherd boy, but the mention of the "house of the Lord" in the closing lines of the poem indicate that the final form of this psalm could not have come from David himself. Scholars understand the individualism of the text and the form of speech (a psalm of trust) to suggest that the psalm is post-exilic, so that what was perhaps a royal prayer was recast after the exile, when the monarchy no longer prevailed.

Structure. The shape of the text is quite simple: vv. 1-4 meditate on God the good shepherd and vv. 5-6 ruminate on God the gracious host. The images of shepherd and host were intimately related in the ancient Near East, and the poem is unified despite its employment of two distinguishable images.

Significance. This psalm is a celebration of the sheer goodness of God. It is surely the best known and most loved of all the psalms. We know this poem so well, most often in the King James Version, that we are in danger of making it profane through familiarity. Indeed, we can purchase posters that pun the poem for amusement. Thus let us recognize and reflect upon the rich images of this psalm.

Behind the images of God as shepherd and God as host is the single idea of God as King. The shepherd metaphor was a common ancient image for the monarch, because it cast him as both leader and provider. Shepherds guide their flocks for a purpose, namely to direct the sheep to the best possible pastures for grazing. Thus leadership is providential in the sense of aiming at making the physical provisions available for undergirding life. Moreover, the shepherd is the source of security for the sheep. There is a positive and a negative side to this idea. Positively, the shepherd establishes peace for the flock by bringing them to the most restful and bountiful setting. Negatively, the shepherd secures the safety of the sheep by warding off any threats to the sheep's well-being. The shepherd's staff both directs and deflects.

The image of host was a natural association of ancient Near Eastern kings who gave occasional extravagant banquets for friends and guests. Thus this image and the image of the shepherd are celebrations of providential provision. Inherent in v. 6 is a kind of primitive eschatology. This comes through in the lines that are normally translated as the statement, "Surely goodness and mercy shall follow me all the days of my life: and I will dwell in the house of the LORD for ever" (KJV), but which may be translated as a declaration of desire, "May only goodness and kindness pursue me all the days of my life, and may I dwell in [or return to] the house of the Lord as long as I live."

Perhaps when using this psalm in worship, one should turn to a truly unfamiliar translation that will cause the congregation to hear the text afresh. The danger will be, however, that only the differences will be heard. In order to minimize this possibility, use of the psalm in an unfamiliar translation as a unison reading may create greater involvement on the part of the congregation.

New Testament Texts

The New Testament texts describe the significance of Jesus in relationship to two very different groups. The redemptive suffering of Jesus is sketched out in I Peter 2:19-25 as an address to slaves, while the protective role of Jesus, as a gate that limits access to the sheep, is explored in John 10:1-10 as an address to religious leaders.

The Epistle: *I Peter 2:19-25*

A Call to Grace

Setting. The audience addressed in I Peter 2:19-25 is stated explicitly in v. 18 as being slaves. This verse should probably be included in the lectionary reading even though it may offend modern sensibility because the writer is not politically sensitive to our agenda for advocating the overthrow of oppressive masters. The setting of slavery is crucial if we are to understand the power of grace-in-suffering that is the central argument of the text.

Structure. I Peter 2:(18) 19-25 separates into two parts: vv. 18-20 are a call for slaves to exhibit God's grace even in the context of unjust suffering, and vv. 21-25 provide a theological basis for such ethical action by interpreting Jesus as God's suffering servant. The text can be outlined in the following manner:

    I. A Call for Grace in Suffering (vv. 18-20)
       A. Address to Slaves (v. 18)
       B. Exposition of Grace: Enduring of Suffering with God as the Object (vv. 19-20)
          1. No value in suffering from just punishment
          2. Wrongful suffering, patiently endured, draws one near to God
    II. Jesus as an Example of Grace in Suffering (vv. 21-25)
       A. Sinless (v. 22)
       B. Did Not Threaten Others in Suffering, but Trusted in God (v. 23)
       C. Bore Our Sins on the Tree (v. 24)
       D. Shepherd (v. 25)

Significance. As noted above, the fact that the writer does not argue against the very institution of slavery presents a hermeneutical problem for modern listeners. An answer to this tension is not to say simply that the writer's world is not our world, for the writer is actually presenting a very radical argument about Christian behavior in this world, namely that Christian conduct cannot be determined by any of the social structures in which we live, but only by Christ. Christ judges all human institutions even while he embodies the grace of God in this world.

Verses 18-20 are a direct address to slaves to follow an ethic of suffering. This is not a call for some form of idealized suffering for its own sake. Three motifs in particular frame the unjust suffering of slaves in a theological context: grace, fear, and consciousness of God. First, the motif of grace (Greek, *charis;* NRSV, "approval") in vv. 19-20 puts unjust suffering in a larger context than the actual experience of it. Grace is a gift from God that allows the slave to endure. In fact the closing reference to grace in v. 20 states that the result of patient endurance of unjust suffering is that it draws the sufferer very near to God (The NRSV translation "you have God's approval" is weak because it does not bring out the spatial imagery of nearness to God). Two additional motifs make clear what the implications of God's grace must be in our perception of situations of suffering, even when those situations are evil. The first attitude is fear in v. 18 (NRSV, "with all deference"). The NRSV translation makes the master the object of the slaves' "fear" (hence the translation, "with all deference"). Fear, however, is a quality that arises in Christians who know the salvation of God (see I Peter 1:17), and not a quality that arises from other persons. The call for fear in the slaves, therefore, is not for the purpose of being good servants but good Christians. This focus on God rather than master is made explicit in v. 19, when the slave is called "to be aware of God" especially in an unjust situation. The ability to endure unjust suffering while focusing on God is grace, which draws the sufferer even nearer to God.

Verses 21-25 provide even more explicit theological background for an ethic of suffering by interpreting the suffering of Jesus in the light of the suffering-servant passage in Isaiah 53. Three aspects of Jesus' ministry and Passion are underscored to show how he is both shepherd and model for Christians who suffer unjustly. First, Jesus committed no sin. Second, Jesus also did not reduce suffering to the immediate experience of it—he did not counter oppression by threatening, rather he trusted in God. Third, the combination of the first two actions of Jesus resulted in his bearing our sins, which frees us also to view suffering from the point of view of grace.

This is a difficult text to preach, especially with the history of race relations in North America, not to mention the Middle East or other oppressive regions. The intended audience and their situation is important in the proclamation of this text. It is not a theological justification for oppression; that is, the audience of the text is not the masters. Rather, it is a theological reflection on evil and how Christians who are victims of evil must act. The central point of the text is that the evil to which we may become victims cannot be allowed to determine the nature of reality for us. God must remain our object of focus in all situations, for then our behavior—itself the result of God's grace—is subversive, because evil will not have ultimate control over us. This is a liberating message, for it means that Christians, both the oppressed and the oppressors, need not remain slaves to evil structures. The place to start the liberating activity is not in the community at large, but in the worshiping congregation, because that is where the power of God is strongest.

The Gospel: *John 10:1-10*

A Parable About Leadership

Setting. After the Prologue in John 1:1-18, the first major section of the Gospel of John is called the Book of Signs. This section extends through chapter 12. A large portion of the Book of Signs explores who Jesus is by comparing him to the major Jewish feasts (John 5, Jesus and Sabbath; John 6, Jesus and Passover; John 7–8, Jesus and Tabernacles; John 10:22-39, Jesus and the Feast of Dedication). John 10:1-10 is part of a larger series of stories (John 9–10:21) about Jesus' teaching and healing after the Feast of Tabernacles. John 9 is an account of Jesus healing a blind man, which results in a confrontation with the Pharisees in John 9:40. This confrontation continues into

141

John 10 and provides the setting for the gospel lesson of this Sunday. Thus we should read John 10:1-10 as being directed to the Pharisees. John 10:1-10, therefore, is a story about leadership in which Jesus contrasts himself to his contemporary religious leaders.

Structure. John 10:1-10 (11-19) separates into two parts. Verses 1-6 include two parables about Jesus and a reaction of unbelief by the religious leaders, vv. 7-10 (11-19) provide an interpretation of the parables. The text can be outlined in the following manner:

I. Two Parables about Leadership (vv. 1-6)
    A. Parable 1: The gate is the only proper way to approach the sheep (vv. 1-3*a*)
    B. Parable 2: The close relationship of the sheep and shepherd (vv. 3*b*-5)
    C. The reaction of unbelief (v. 6)
II. The Interpretation of the Parables (vv. 7-19)
    A. The interpretation of the gate in the first parable (vv. 7-10)
II. B. The interpretation of the shepherd in the second parable (vv. 11-18)

The outline illustrates how vv. 1-10 are part of a larger text and how the more limited text of the lectionary requires that we focus on the first parable about the gate and not the second parable about the relationship of the sheep and shepherd. This is a problem because the question of Christian leadership that is behind the parables requires that we look at Jesus as both gate and shepherd, and thus extend the text through v. 18.

Significance. The central question for preaching this text is how Jesus provides us with a model of leadership in the Church through the imagery of gate and shepherd. The first parable provides the structure from which leadership must evolve, while the second parable provides the content of Christian leadership.

In the first parable, Jesus states that the gate is the only proper way to approach the sheep. Jesus provides two interpretations of the gate in vv. 7-10. Both interpretations are statements about himself. First, in vv. 7-8 Jesus states that he is the only gate through which any leader/shepherd must approach the sheep. Any other method of approaching the sheep is robbery. Second, in vv. 9-10 Jesus expands on the first conclusion. Jesus is the only way to approach the sheep because he is the sole door of salvation. This parable shows us the road to leadership in the Church, but it does not provide the content of Christian leadership. It leaves us with the question of how the one who passes through the gate is transformed so that the sheep instinctively know him or her.

The interpretation to the second parable in vv. 11-18 provides an answer to our question. The content of Christian leadership comprises two parts: (1) the shepherd is willing to die for the sheep (vv. 11-13), and (2) the shepherd knows all of the sheep.

The central point of this text for preaching is that the structure out of which Christian leadership must emerge is Jesus, and that anyone who passes through Jesus must reflect the content of his ministry. The gospel writer states further that when this two-part process of structure and content happens, we, the Church, will instinctively know leadership. The proof of the effectiveness of this conclusion really lies in our epistle for this Sunday. As the Church, we know that in spite of the master-slave relationship of I Peter 2:(18) 19-25 it is really the slaves who embody leadership in that context. Suffering unjustly for the sake of God rather than self can only be done by someone who has passed through the gate of Jesus and absorbed the content of his ministry. This is leadership in the Church, and we instinctively know it.

Easter 4: The Celebration

Today's epistle provides an opportunity to discuss what it means to "live liturgically" by offering our lives and our suffering in an intentional way to God. So much recent discussion has centered around worship as "celebration" that many of its other aspects have been diminished, aspects that might help balance the definition of worship as "party hats and balloons."

We model in the eucharistic liturgy and prayer what it means to live as an offering in the world. Many eucharistic prayers have a section referred to (technically) as the oblation, where specific mention is made of Christ's sacrifice and our own self-sacrifice as his disciples.

For example, the United Methodists now pray, "We offer ourselves in praise and thanksgiving as a holy and living sacrifice, in union with Christ's offering for us."

Our modern world thinks of suffering as something to be remedied. Christian faith also thinks of it as something to be offered. St. Augustine said that Christ's sufferings "are complete, but in him as head; there remain even now the sufferings of Christ to be endured in the body." It is here that the priesthood of the laity finds additional meaning, because the function of priesthood is to offer sacrifice. Parts of two of Wesley's poems make the point.

First, we offer our self-sacrifice with Christ, because we have been baptized into his body.

> Shall we let our God groan
> And suffer alone?
> Or to Calvary fly,
> And nobly resolve with our Master to die?
>
> His servants shall be
> With him on the tree,
> Where Jesus was slain
> His crucified servants shall always remain.

Second, because we have been baptized into Christ, all aspects of our lives become an offering to God and Christ is there to support us in our efforts.

> Thee may I set at my right hand,
> Whose eyes mine inmost substance see,
> And labor on at thy command,
> And offer all my works to thee.

Fifth Sunday of Easter

Texts from Acts and Psalms

The lesson from Acts tells of the stoning of Stephen. The psalm has no actual connection with Stephen's speech or the account of his execution, but in the story of his death Stephen prays. Psalm 31 is itself a prayer-song for deliverance from one's enemies in which the psalmist utters a line (31:5) similar to Stephen's first prayer (7:59), so there is an imaginative way to relate the texts to each other.

The Lesson: *Acts 7:55-60*

Living and Dying as Jesus Did

Setting. The pattern of story-telling in Acts is to narrate a specific event, often in some detail, to the point of reporting speeches and statements made by prominent persons. Then Acts will give a general summary statement about the situation of the believers that reveals the progress of the early Christians in spreading the gospel. This Sunday's lesson occurs in Acts 6:1–8:8, a large unit of material with the following sub-units: the appointment of the seven (6:1-7), the arrest of Stephen (6:8–7:1), Stephen's speech (7:2-53), Stephen's execution/ murder (7:54–8:1), the subsequent persecution of the Church (8:1-3), and the extension of the gospel outside Jerusalem to Judea and Samaria (8:4-8). Thus the story of the murder of Stephen comes immediately after his elaborate, important speech and as a consequence of his remarks. And this incident immediately precedes and leads to the subsequent persecution of the Church which, in turn, actually advanced the proclamation of the gospel.

Beginning the lesson at v. 55 does not give sufficient information to explain the hostility of the crowd toward Stephen. A free retelling of the story in Acts 6:8–7:2 prior to the reading of the lesson or expanding the lesson to include 7:54 will help put the text in a sensible context.

Structure. The scene is narrated from a third-person point of view with an alternating focus on Stephen and the Jerusalem Jews. In the lesson proper, vv. 55-56 focus on Stephen; vv. 57-58 focus on the Jerusalem Jews; and verses 59-60 focus, again, on Stephen.

Significance. Perhaps the most striking feature of this tragic story is the numerous parallels between this brief account and the scenes of the Lukan Passion narrative. The suffering and death of Jesus provide a model for recounting Stephen's death. The parallels are even more striking when viewed as part of a larger pattern of parallels: Jesus and Stephen are tried before the Jewish council on charges brought by false witnesses. Under fire from their opponents, both speak of ''the Son of Man''; indeed, other than Jesus, Stephen is the only New Testament character ever to employ this title. On the cross Jesus commits his spirit into the hands of his ''Father''; whereas while Stephen is being stoned he says, ''Lord Jesus, receive my spirit.'' While he is dying (there is a famous textual problem in the Greek here), Jesus prays, ''Father, forgive them; for they know not what they do''; and as he expires, Stephen cries out, ''Lord, do not hold this sin against them.'' And the deaths of both Jesus and Stephen result in the spreading of the gospel. A much longer list is possible, but these items show the deliberate parallels in these stories. A sermon could use these parallels to develop the theme, ''living and dying as Jesus did.'' In such reflection, one can consider other ways in which Jesus Christ provides a model for believers to follow. The one danger in such reflection will be to reduce Jesus simply to functioning as a model for our lives. Against that temptation we recall two things: First, remember that the Church long ago judged the ''exemplarist Christology'' of Peter Abelard to be inadequate! Second, the text itself will not support a move to view Jesus only as an example or model to be followed. As Stephen stands debating and kneels dying, he looks into the heavens, and through the power of the Holy Spirit, he has a vision of Jesus, whom he calls ''Lord'' and refers to as ''the Son of Man''; moreover, he prays to Jesus, understanding that his petitions are heard by the one whom he follows in life and death, and whom he trusts he will follow in resurrection.

Another way to avoid reducing Jesus to the level of mere model is to develop the sermon by focusing on Stephen as a model: In the face of danger, he remains true to his Lord, testifying to the fault of the people and the truth of the gospel. Rejected by others he knows himself to be in fellowship with the risen Christ. Having been a faithful witness, he is filled with the compassion of Christ, and trusting the risen Jesus, he even prays for those who kill him. As Stephen follows Jesus Christ, he provides us with a model for living freely and faithfully as Jesus' followers.

The Response: *Psalm 31:1-8, 15-16*

Help, in a Hurry Lord!

Setting. Interpreters agree this is an individual lament psalm, but they offer different analyses of its inner structure. Clearly the lesson from the lectionary understands vv. 1-8 as the first of a series of three cries for deliverance (vv. 1-8 [from enemies], vv. 9-12 [from illness], vv. 13-18 [from enemies]) followed by a thanksgiving for the Lord's grace (vv. 19-24).

Structure. Verses 1-5 form a petition for deliverance. Verse 6 declares both the Lord's ways and the psalmist's trust in God. Then, vv. 7-8 express the psalmist's joy in experiencing the extrication for which vv. 1-5 asked. Verses 15-16 are a statement of full confidence in God and God's power to save.

Significance. This psalm is a powerful appeal for divine preservation and vindication. It is familiar to us because in the Lukan Passion narrative Jesus utters part of v. 6 as he is dying on the cross (Luke 23:46).

The psalm takes up a major theme of appeal in the entire Psalter: "refuge." The idea of seeking refuge in the Lord expresses the desire for security or vindication from God. The psalmist is concerned that he or she not be shamed. For the ancients, matters of honor and shame were of ultimate importance. Our individualistic culture is equally

147

concerned with personal success and failure, but the more communal, clannish, or tribal mind-set of ancients made honor and shame key conditions of human behavior. This is more than having egg on one's face or spilling soup on one's lap; to be shamed was to lose both one's self-esteem and one's derived esteem in the larger social group. To be shamed would open one to ridicule, even from former friends and family members.

Remarkably the psalmist understands the basis of delivery from shame to be the Lord's righteousness. God is faithful to those who call on him. The psalmist does not bother to muster a list of merits to justify the appeal (even the declaration in v. 6 is not a motivation for God's assistance); rather, making the appeal to God is turning to the one who is faithful. Indeed, the psalmist does not hesitate to turn to the Lord to ask for a quick response ("rescue me speedily," v. 2). The psalmist assumes that God is capable of a swift answer, so this psalm asks for one.

Verses 3-5 present a series of three powerful images. First, v. 3 offers a meditation on God as the psalmist's rock and fortress. These images are further evidence of the psalmist's confidence in God's capacity to protect from danger. Second, v. 4 informs us indirectly that the psalmist's danger may be more a potential than an actual threat. The reference to the net is common language, but the metaphor suggests that the net is hidden and not in plain sight. Nevertheless, at the perception of possible danger, the psalmist turns to God as the source of security. How can we understand the move toward God when one merely suspects there may be problems ahead? The third metaphor in v. 5 tells us, saying, "Into your hand I commit my spirit; you have redeemed me, O Lord, faithful God." The psalmist entrusts his or her whole being or life to God, because God has already redeemed him or her. The psalmist's unflinching trust of God as redeemer comes about because God is known as such. This is no blind leap of faith but an action based on previous experience.

Verse 6 forms a contrast between those involved with false gods (the perceived enemies?) and the psalmist who trusts in God. Somewhat unexpectedly, vv. 7-8 celebrate the very deliverance for which the psalmist appealed in vv. 1-4. Remarkably, in v. 2 the psalmist asked God to act with speed, and apparently the prayer was answered! Thus the statement of confidence (vv. 15-16) was not unfounded.

This psalm is a model of bold prayer in full trust with no hesitation. In worship we should let this reading be a vehicle to guide us into ready, forthright prayer.

New Testament Texts

Both New Testament texts for this Sunday focus on the meaning of Jesus in the light of his Resurrection. First Peter 2:2-10 explores the character of the risen Lord in the post-Resurrection age with the feminine imagery of mother's milk and the architectural metaphor of a living stone. John 14:1-14 describes the relationship in the Godhead of the Son and the Father, and the implications of this relationship on the life of Jesus' disciples.

The Epistle: *I Peter 2:2-10*

Being Breast-fed into a Living Stone

Setting. The Epistle for this Sunday cuts across two texts that are not closely related in I Peter. First Peter 2:1-3 provides a conclusion to an exhortation to holiness that began in I Peter 1:13. The focus of this section is to describe the growing relationship of the audience (newly converted Christians) with Jesus and the Father. A number of relational words are used: the audience is addressed as "obedient children" (1:14), who have been "born anew" (1:23) through the word of God—which unlike grass will not fade away. First Peter 2:1-3 provides a conclusion to this emerging relationship (that the audience has been born anew) first, with an ethical command in v. 1 ("rid yourselves of all malice and all guile . . . "), and, second, with an analogy of infants being breast-fed with spiritual milk in vv. 2-3. First Peter 2:4-10 shifts the discussion to the architectural imagery of Zion. Here the focus is more on the new reality that has been ushered in with Jesus' Resurrection than on the relationship of God and the people of God per se. As will become more evident when we look further at the structure and significance of I Peter 2:2-10, it may be necessary for the preacher to make a decision about which aspect of the text will be the focus for a sermon: the new emerging relationship of God and believer (vv. 1-3) or the new reality (the kingdom of God) that has been ushered in through the Resurrection of Jesus (vv. 4-10).

Structure. First Peter 2:(1) 2-10 can be outlined in the following manner:

I. The Milk of Jesus (vv. 1-3)
   A. Negative Command: Put Away Slander, etc. (v. 1)
   B. Positive Command (vv. 2-3)
      1. Continue Breast Feeding on Spiritual Milk
      2. Grow Up to Salvation
II. Jesus as the "Living Stone" (vv. 4-10)
   A. Introductory Invitation (vv. 4-5)
      1. Come to Jesus, the Living Stone
      2. Be a Living Stone
   B. The New Reality of Jesus as a Living Stone
      1. A New Foundation in Zion (v. 6) (Isaiah 28:16)
      2. The Results to Unbeliever and Believer
         a. Unbeliever (vv. 7-8) (Psalm 118:22; Isaiah 8:14)
         b. Believer (vv. 9-10) (Exodus 19:5-6)

Significance. First Peter 2:2-10 is about new salvific relationships and a new order for reality (the Kingdom of God) in the post-Easter world.

First, salvation is a surprising reversal of our experience, which is out of our control. Because salvation is out of our control, it is both liberating and threatening. The primary event of salvation in the Old Testament, the Exodus, provides an example. The Exodus is liberating, for it is a radical reversal of social order—the slaves are freed from the Egyptians. The Exodus, however, is also threatening to Israel, for the radical reversal of social order does not result in freedom from all relationships. Instead, Israel's dependence on Egypt is shifted to dependence on God. They are like an infant in the wilderness, who must be fed in a special way by God—through miraculous gifts of water and manna. The social and relational reversals that Israel experienced in the Exodus are the equivalent to the use of the image of rebirth by the author of I Peter. Central to this vision of salvation is the rejection of the idea of liberation as freedom. Rebirth means, rather, that we shift all of our dependencies onto God. We become vulnerable like infants, and we must be breast-fed by God to live at all. This intimate image defines our new relationship with God in the wake of the Resurrection of Jesus.

Second, the new order of reality in the post-Easter world is apparent because I Peter 2:4-10 is less concerned with describing the intimate and dependent relationship that we have with God, and more interested in outlining the content of salvation. What is new in a world that exists after the Resurrection of Jesus? The author argues that only one thing is new, namely that Jesus inaugurates a new foundation for Zion (v. 6). The imagery of Zion is primarily the language of creation and God's presence in it. By using the imagery of Zion, the author of I Peter is stating that Jesus has, by his ministry and passion, ushered in a new world order (the Kingdom of God), in which God is present in a new way. Humans are not the primary focus in v. 6, rather creation is. The kingdom of God, however, cannot help effecting what it means to be human, and this becomes the secondary concern of the writer in vv. 7-10. The new world order will become an obstacle to those who do not see it (vv. 7-8). In contrast, those who see the new world order and enter into it will be transformed (vv. 9-10). The writer picks up motifs from Exodus 19:5-6, where Israel was also described as being qualitatively changed because of the breaking in of God into this world at Mount Sinai. The qualitative change of holiness gives rise to new function in this world, namely, to declare the breaking in of God's kingdom, which is a place where we are free to be absolutely dependent on God like newborn, breast-fed babies.

The Gospel: *John 14:1-14*

Jesus and His Church

Setting. John 14:1-14 is the first part of Jesus' closing discourse to his disciples. The question addressed in this speech is relational—that is, how will Jesus be present with his disciples after he has left them. Thus John 14:1-14 returns to the topic of the first section of I Peter—namely, the relationship between the risen Lord and his disciples. In the Gospel text, the relationship of Jesus to his disciples is explored more explicitly in the context of worship by presenting a reinterpretation of the Deuteronomistic theology of naming the presence of God. This Deuteronomistic theology arose in ancient Israel out of the belief that God would be present in any place of worship where his name was called. The account of Solomon's prayer in I Kings 8 during the dedication of the Temple provides illustration of this theology. Note how frequently Solomon states that even though God dwells in heaven and not on earth, nevertheless, when God's name is called upon in worship, God would be present with Israel. Here we see an emerging theology of worship that emphasizes the importance of proclamation. The calling upon God (most probably on the basis of Scripture) actually becomes a channel for God to be present in worship. In John 14:1-14, this calling on God as a channel for God to be present in worship revolves around the name of Jesus.

Structure. John 14:1-14 is difficult to outline, and you will see that commentators branch off in a number of different directions. In order to investigate the developing theology for naming Jesus, we will look at the passage in three sections, which can be outlined as follows:

    I. Jesus is the place (vv. 1-3)
    II. Jesus is the way (vv. 4-11)
    III. Jesus is the name (vv. 12-14)

Significance. Verses 1-3 introduce the problem that is giving rise to the speech. How will Jesus be present with his disciples? This problem is assumed in the opening words of comfort, "Do not let your hearts be troubled." These words lead immediately into a discussion of "place." Jesus is going to his Father's house, which has many rooms, and once there he will "prepare a place" for his disciples. The imagery in this speech is very eschatological, and upon first reading it appears to be very otherworldly and future oriented—the Father's house is someplace else (presumably heaven), and Jesus is going there to prepare for a future return. The explicit use of "place," however, should caution us about removing this discourse too far from the here and now of our world, because the use of "place" is very important in the Deuteronomistic theology, where it is used frequently in conjunction with "the name." For example, "the place of the name" signifies the presence of God with the worshiping community in I Kings 8:29, 35. Thus "the place of the name" is not an otherworldly, future reality but the presence of God here and now in the worshiping community. The use of this motif in John 14, where the imminent absence of Jesus is the central concern, suggests that the present worshiping community may also be the focus of vv. 1-3.

Two questions—one by Thomas and another by Philip—in vv. 5-11 move the discussion even more explicitly into the present time by exploring how Jesus is both a place, and a "way" in which disciples must move. Thomas asks how disciples can know the way of Jesus? Jesus' response is that his very person is in fact the way to God. Philip then follows with a question concerning the relationship of Jesus and the Father, to which Jesus responds that, from the point of view of the disciples, there is little distinction. To follow in the way of Jesus is to know the Father.

The close interrelationship of Jesus and the Father leads to a theology of the name of Jesus in vv. 12-14, which provides an answer to the opening question of how Jesus will be present with his disciples in the post-Resurrection age. Whoever believes in Jesus and follows in his way has the power of the name of Jesus. What this means practically is that calling upon God (through the name of Jesus) becomes a channel for the risen Lord to be present with the worshiping community. This theology of the name of Jesus will be difficult to communicate in preaching, because it appears magical when preachers and evangelists invoke privileged access in order to manipulate their God. Yet the point of the text is precisely that the name of Jesus has special power for the Christian. Thus one task in preaching this text will be to convey how all of our conversations with God presuppose a special power in the name of Jesus, as the standard liturgical conclusion to our prayers indicates, "In the name of Jesus, Amen."

Easter 5: The Celebration

In the sanctoral cycle of the more catholic churches, St. Stephen's Day (made famous by the song for Good King Wenceslaus) is December 26, so one suspects that little or no attention gets paid to the suffering of that protomartyr on the day following Christmas Day. Today, the preacher can remedy that situation, provided it is remembered that when the Church celebrates the witness of a saint (or all the saints on November 1) what is really being celebrated is the work of Christ in that person. This point is made in the phrasing of the collect for St. Stephen's Day in the *Lutheran Book of Worship*: "Grant us grace, O Lord, that like Stephen we may learn to love even our enemies and seek forgiveness for those who desire our hurt." What is effective is God's grace working through us. The preacher might wish to underscore the fact that the Greek word for witness is the root of our English word *martyr*, and to explore some of the implications of that for the Easter faith. If our identification with the death of Christ was not pursued via last week's epistle, the example of Stephen can open the way for it now. Worship leaders might rummage around through some old hymnals and resurrect the hymn "The Son of God Goes Forth to War," with its eloquent second stanza:

> The martyr first, whose eagle eye
> Could pierce beyond the grave,
> Who saw his Master in the sky,
> And called on him to save:
> Like him, with pardon on his tongue,
> In midst of mortal pain
> He prayed for them that did the wrong:
> Who follows in his train?

Today's prayers might also include a litany of the martyrs: a list of men and women who have given their lives for the faith over the centuries. The litany should include the name and some indication of the grace or witness made evident in the particular death.

The epistle suggests the use of the following collect:

> Almighty God, you have built your Church upon the foundation of the apostles and prophets, Jesus Christ himself being the chief cornerstone. Grant us so to be joined together in unity of spirit by their teaching that we may be made a holy temple acceptable to you.

The Lutheran hymn, "Built on the Rock the Church Shall Stand," is one which deserves wider recognition. It would make an excellent response to today's epistle.

The Gospel today will be familiar to many hearers only from the funeral service. This can provide an opening for discussing why Christian funerals are Easter celebrations. The witness of Stephen in the first lesson may be connected to the witness that contemporary believers can make by their funerals, if not by their dying! Here may be an opportunity to preach about the character of a Christian funeral and to encourage people to plan their services in advance as a final witness that they will want to make about their faith.

Sixth Sunday of Easter

Texts from Acts and Psalms

If there is logic to the selection or combination of these texts, it is not readily discernible, even by stretching one's imagination. The sermon-speech by Paul in Acts works out a kind of "crisis-theology," which insists that necessary changes are currently demanded by the work of God in Jesus Christ. The psalm is a profound expression of piety, filled with vivid imagery and recalling the goodness of God both to Israel and to the psalmist.

The Lesson: *Acts 17:22-31*

The Changing of the Times

Setting. The lesson is the well-known speech by Paul on the Areopagus, or "Mars Hill." Having come from Asia Minor to Europe (the Roman province Macedonia), Paul and his colleagues, Timothy and Barnabas, moved through Philippi, Thessalonica, and Beroea before arriving in Athens. Paul was left alone there while the others returned to work with congregations that they had previously founded. Before Paul's address, vv. 16-21 set the stage. Paul was provoked by the idols throughout Athens, and he proceeded to argue the case of his gospel both in the synagogue and in the marketplace. He became embroiled in a controversy with Epicurean and Stoic philosophers, who wanted to hear about Jesus and "anastasis"—literally, *resurrection* in Greek, but the hearers take this feminine Greek word as the name of a goddess, so that Paul is thought to proclaim a new divine couple. Acts 17:21 informs us of the legendary character of the Athenians, who "would spend their time in nothing but telling or hearing something new.'' After Paul's speech, vv. 32-34 report the outcomes: mockery, curiosity, and belief.

Structure. Interpreters sometimes point to the ''sense-parallels'' between this speech and I Thessalonians 1:9-10; both start with the idea of knowledge of the one true God who now demands repentance that is based on Christ's Resurrection and oriented to the final judgment. The reported speech can be analyzed more specifically, however. Verses 22-23 are a kind of flattering introduction designed to win the goodwill of the hearers. Then, vv. 24-25 declare the person and nature of God. Verses 26-29 work out a progressive argument, moving from God's work, to God's purposes, to our (human) relationship to God, to our proper regard for God. Verse 30 declares the change of times, which demands repentance; and v. 31 declares the positive and negative dimension of judgment through the risen Jesus.

Significance. The presentation of Paul in this passage does not so much show him arguing as proclaiming. This speech has only loose associations with normal Pauline theology, and indeed, when read only in part, one could garner a strange idea of what Paul thought about God and humanity. Parts of the speech sound vaguely more like Stoic pantheism than Christian theology. Lest we take a side street and get lost by examining some of the exceptional ideas in these lines, we should notice that the speech rambles to a thoroughly christological conclusion. In fact, a concern with Christology was the occasion of this speech (see 17:18). Thus we should follow Acts's lead and begin where the speech ends.

Paul's speech is a radical critique of pagan polytheism. He focuses on the Resurrection of Jesus Christ as the decisive act of God, which negates the value of general human religiosity. God's raising of Jesus so precisely revealed the power of God that it demanded that humans turn away from all other celebrations of the divine in order to concentrate on what God had shown to be central. This speech does not elaborate the content of the true religion to which God calls humanity in and through the Resurrection, so we cannot work out a theology of revelation or redemption from this text alone. But the passage does identify the crucial place of Jesus Christ in God's work. We learn that the raising of Jesus promises that God has set a day for judgment. This is not merely a threat but also a promise. Judgment issues the gift of salvation as well as the purification of punishment. The portrait of God in the odd lines of the speech leading up to the declaration about Jesus should not be pressed out literally or even too far. Instead, we may recognize that they speak of God as one who gives without taking, as one who is generous in nature. Yet, the Resurrection of Jesus is taken to mean that now, with God, not everything goes. In short, because God has acted overtly in raising Jesus, we now have a standard whereby we can critique and abandon previous efforts to express the ineffable character of God. Before the Resurrection, God was lenient, but the speech declares that now the times have changed. Therefore, the call is to repentance, which, by implication, means the affirmation of the one true God and what God has done, is doing, and will do in Jesus Christ.

In the pluralistic currents of contemporary society, this text may cause more problems than it solves. What looks like another illustration of the diversity of canonical models for thinking and talking about God turns out to be one of the most narrowly focused claims in scripture. Coming to terms with the complex content and the pointed tone of this passage may be difficult, but it will reward those who wrestle with the issues it raises.

The Response: *Psalm 66:8-20*

Double-Barreled Piety

Setting. This is a complex psalm, which may have been prepared for use by a relatively affluent person who came to the Temple to discharge vows that he or she had made. The fatlings, rams, bulls, and goats in vv. 13-15 were exceptional sacrifices, the cost of which were far beyond the means of everyday people. The setting indicated by the language of v. 8 is that of an assembly. Although we cannot discern the precise nature of the suffering amidst which the psalmist made the vow, we see that the vow was made in difficult circumstances, which are now past.

Structure. By beginning this lesson at v. 8, the lectionary recognizes the distinction between the materials in vv. 1-7 and the remainder of the psalm. In fact, vv. 1-7 are a highly poetic, perhaps hymnic, statement of divine praise. Then, vv. 8-20 fall into two parts: vv. 8-12 form a statement of communal praise ("our," "us," "we"), and vv. 13-20 are an individual's thanksgiving in the context of the assembly ("I," "my" and "Come and hear, all you who fear God").

Significance. Verses 8-12 recall God's preservation of Israel through not one but many difficulties. Much of the language of this section evokes images of Egypt, the Exodus, and the entry into the promised land. Yet, the psalmist may have an even broader sweep of Israel's story in mind. Remarkable are the difficulties faced by the nation and interpreted here as "trials" or "tests." God's purpose in bringing the people through these difficulties is to refine them. Exactly how much credit goes to God as the initiator of the trials is not clear, although God is envisioned here as fully sovereign rather than merely as a sustainer ("You, O God, have tested us . . . You brought us into the net; you laid burdens . . . you let people ride over our heads . . . yet you have brought us out . . . "). The capacity of the ancient Israelite mind to acknowledge God as sovereign Lord, without being moved to sheer bitterness, is amazing. Indeed, this psalm is a celebration of God's goodness, not a complaint about God's capriciousness or injustice!

The last verses of the psalm allow the psalmist to step forth from the assembly to address God directly in thanksgiving and to tell the assembly what God has done. The combination of thanksgiving and proclamation is prominent and powerful. The psalm combines practice and preaching, so that the testimony takes on a force beyond mere deed or mere word. This example of piety is a model for all of us who earnestly desire to praise and serve God. "Practice what you preach" is an old maxim, but its truth cannot be exhausted.

New Testament Texts

Both New Testament texts address ways in which Jesus is present with post-Easter Christians. First Peter 3:13-22 explores how baptism allows Christians to live in the Spirit of Jesus even at times of suffering, while John 14:15-21 describes how the Holy Spirit dwells in disciples as an extension of Jesus.

The Epistle: *I Peter 3:13-22*

Being Saved Through Baptism

Setting. The theme of unjust suffering continues in I Peter 3:13-22. As we have seen in previous lessons from I Peter, the author encourages his audience to endure unjust suffering and then offers Jesus as an example. The situation of the present believers and the past action of Jesus is brought together at the end of the passage through a discussion of baptism. Baptism is presented as a link between Jesus and present believer, which provides the power for Christians to endure even unjust suffering.

Structure. I Peter 3:13-22 separates into two parts. The first part, vv. 13-17, is a direct address to the audience, describing how they must act in the context of suffering. The second part, vv. 18-22, shifts the focus from present suffering to the Passion of Jesus in order to provide a theological framework for believers to endure unjust suffering in the present time. The passage can be outlined in the following way:

I. The Promise of Blessing Even in Suffering (vv. 13-17)
  A. Question: Who Can Harm You, If You Are Zealous for Good? (v. 13)
  B. Answer: No One
    1. First Exhortation (vv. 14-15*a*)
       Do not fear persecutor/Sanctify Jesus in your hearts
    2. Second Exhortation (vv. 15*b*-16)
       Make an account of your hope/Fear God with good conscience
  C. Summary: Better to Suffer for Good Than for Evil, If It Is God's Will (v. 17)

   II. The Reason Why There Can Be Blessing Even in Suffering
      (vv. 18-22)
     A. Jesus Died in the Flesh (v. 18*a*)
     B. Jesus Lives in the Spirit (v. 18*b*)
     C. The Journey of Jesus to Heaven and the Meaning of
        Baptism (vv. 19-22)
       1. Noah was saved through the flood
       2. Present Christians are saved through baptism

Significance. Upon first looking at the outline of I Peter 3:13-22 it
appears to separate clearly into a call to ethical action, followed by a
theological rationale for action. Upon closer examination, however,
the separation is not so stark. The summary in v. 17 makes it clear that
suffering in and of itself is not being idealized, and furthermore, that
the sufferer is not allowed to make the determination of what
constitutes unjust suffering. Note the qualifier in this verse, ''if it is
God's will.'' This summary statement makes it clear that unjust
suffering for Christians cannot be determined simply by our
employing sociological or psychological criteria but that it requires
theological criteria. In other words, we are not reliable for
determining what constitutes unjust suffering. So how do we know
when suffering is in fact God's will, and thus something that we must
endure? Two motifs in the first section of the lesson point us in the
right direction, and both imply revelation. The writer tells us that in
order to know unjust suffering we must have a proper fear of God in
the present that is firmly rooted in knowing what is, in fact, our hope.

The second part of the lesson (vv. 18-22) outlines what our hope is
by reviewing the Passion of Jesus and how we go about knowing the
will of God in the present time through baptism. The Passion of Jesus
separates into three parts: Jesus died in the flesh as the result of unjust
suffering (v. 18*a*), lives in the Spirit (v. 18*b*), and has journeyed to
heaven (vv. 19-22). Jesus' life in the Spirit sets up a contrast between
the past salvation of Noah and the present salvation of Christians,
which allows the writer to explore the meaning of baptism.

What is the nature of the analogy? The analogy is not simply the
water of the flood and the water of baptism. Rather, the analogy is

the salvation of Noah and his family through water and the salvation of Christians through baptism. The analogy underscores how baptism is not a psychological rite of passage but quite literally the movement from one world to another—as the ark carried Noah's family through the flood to another world. Entering this new world through baptism affects the believer, for it applies the benefits of Christ's death and Resurrection to us, which results in spiritual transformation. In other words, we see the world differently in baptism—with a clear conscience or to use a Pauline term, a transformed mind—because we have, in fact, entered a different world of which the Church is the first emerging sign. It is only when we have two feet firmly planted in this new world—the kingdom ushered in by Jesus which is being made manifest through his Church—that we know (1) what our hope is, (2) what proper fear of God entails (and why we need not fear any other power), and, finally, (3) what constitutes unjust suffering. The central point of I Peter is that only the Church as a whole can decide what is unjust suffering. We as individuals cannot perform this task, and it is our baptism that makes this point clear, for it is a collective sacrament, which grafts each of us into the body of the Church.

The Gospel: *John 14:15-21*

The Presence of Jesus in the Spirit

Setting. John 14:15-21 is an extension of the last discourse of Jesus in the Gospel of John, the beginning of which was our lesson for last Sunday. In John 14:1-14, Jesus began to address the question of how he would be present with his disciples after he left them. John 14:15-21 continues to address the question by exploring how Jesus and the Paraclete (Holy Spirit) are interrelated.

Structure. We should note that John 14:15-21 is part of a larger discourse that extends at least through v. 24. The importance of making this note is that it underscores how the larger text of vv. 15-24 actually explores the relationship of the Spirit (vv. 15-17), Jesus (vv. 18-21), and the Father (vv. 22-24). The lesson for this Sunday does not explore in detail the relationship of Jesus and the Father (although it is mentioned in vv. 20-21), but focuses instead on the relationship of Jesus and the Spirit. The more limited text of vv. 15-21 can be outlined in the following manner:

I. The Spirit Will Be with the Disciples (vv. 15-17)
   A. Love Jesus and Keep His Commandments (v. 15)
   B. The Sending of the Paraclete/Spirit (vv. 16-17)
      1. World cannot see
      2. Disciples see
II. Jesus Will Be with the Disciples (vv. 18-21)
   A. The Presence of Jesus (vv. 18-20)
      1. World will not see
      2. Disciples will see and live
   B. Keeping Jesus' Commandments Is Loving Him (v. 21)

Significance. Three issues stand out in this text. The first is the importance of the Paraclete or Holy Spirit in the life of the Church; the second is the new perception of the world that results from having the indwelling of the Spirit; and the third is that the presence of the Spirit in disciples will result in loving action.

First, the importance of the Paraclete for the life of the Church. There are five passages about the Paraclete in John, of which todays lesson is the first (14:15-17, 26; 15:26-27; 16:7-11, 12-14). Scholars who have studied the role of the Paraclete in John suggest that there are two distinct, but interrelated functions of the Spirit. One function of the Paraclete is to be an extension of Jesus in his physical absence. In this role, the Spirit dwells in the disciples of Jesus, teaches them about Jesus, comforts them, and guides them in this present world. The first part of John 14:15-21 explores this role of the Paraclete as the counselor (v. 16), as the source of truth (v. 17), as an indwelling presence of the risen Jesus (v. 17).

Second, there is a new perception of the world that results from the indwelling of the Paraclete. Both parts of John 14:15-21 develop this theme. In v. 17 we are told that the world cannot receive the Spirit; only the disciples can grasp its presence. This argument continues into v. 19 where we are told that the world cannot even see the Spirit. Instead, it is the reality open only to the disciples of Jesus.

Third, a new ethic arises when we enter the new world that was ushered in with Jesus. The new ethic is that we love Jesus and keep his commandments. This command actually frames our text by occurring in vv. 15 and 21.

These three issues in John 14:15-21 underscore how the Spirit has a two-sided role in this world: to teach disciples about Jesus and to judge the world. This two-sided function means that the presence of the risen Lord in the form of the Spirit necessarily brings about division in our world, not because people are being judged psychologically or sociologically, but because in Christ, God has ushered in the kingdom. The Spirit is our door into this world, and this fact links the Gospel back to the topic of baptism in I Peter 3:13-22, for this sacrament is our link to the Spirit. We see the world differently after baptism, because we have, in fact, entered a different world, of which the Church is the first manifestation.

Easter 6: The Celebration

Reference is made to the use of the Apostles' Creed throughout Easter as a reminder of our baptism, because it is the Church's ancient baptismal creed. Today's epistle contains something like an affirmation of faith, and it contains an allusion to baptism as well. It could be cast into a congregational act of worship for use as today's creedal statement.

In gentleness and reverence
let us make our defense of the hope that is in us.

**Christ suffered for sins once for all,
the righteous for the unrighteous,
in order to bring us to God.
He was put to death in the flesh, but made alive in the spirit,
in which he went and made a proclamation
to the spirits in prison,
who in former times did not obey,
when God waited patiently in the days of Noah,
during the building of the ark,
in which eight persons were saved through water.**

**and baptism now saves us
through the Resurrection of Jesus Christ,
who has gone into heaven
and is at the right hand of God,
with angels, authorities and powers
made subject to him.**

(Dozeman's adaptation of I Pet. 3:15b-22, NRSV)

If the Apostles' Creed is used with its reference to the descent to the dead, this text can be used as a way of exploring that dogma. Given that this coming Thursday will be Ascension Day, the text can help proclaim the total Lordship of Christ by its portrayal of him among the dead and among the angels.

The following Wesley text is a fitting response to the reading of today's Gospel. It can be sung to the tune St. Catherine.

Spirit of truth, essential God,
Wno didst thine ancient saints inspire,
Shed in their hearts thy love abroad
And touch their hallowed lips with fire;
Our God from all eternity,
World without end we worship thee.

*From *Hymns and Psalms: A Methodist and Ecumenical Hymn Book* (London: Methodist Publishing House, 1983), no. 480.

Seventh Sunday of Easter

Texts from Acts and Psalms

The texts from Acts 1 and Psalm 68 have no overt parallel motif that would cast them into a prophecy-fulfillment scheme. Yet strikingly, both passages assume a common, profoundly biblical point of view of God's Reign. In Acts 1 the Ascension means that the Jesus of the past is the risen Lord of the present, who through the Ascension moves into a position to return as the Lord of the future. In turn, Psalm 68 celebrates the kingship of God by recalling the Lord's past saving activities, God's present grace, and by looking forward to what God will do to achieve the standards of righteousness in the future.

The Lesson: *Acts 1:6-14*

The One Who Was, Is, and Shall Be

Setting. The lesson focuses on the Ascension of Jesus and the events that transpired in relation to it. Verses 6-14 are part of the introductory portion of Acts, which covers the time from Easter to Pentecost and comprises the whole of Acts 1. Above all, this chapter of Acts establishes the continuity of everything that follows with all that preceded in the Gospel according to Luke. The ministry that the disciples undertake is the direct result of the commission that Jesus gives them in Acts 1. Both the power for and the direction of their work are from the Holy Spirit, which comes upon them as Jesus promises, again, in Acts 1. Thus there is no absolute distinction between the work that Jesus began and the work that the disciples do, or better, continue.

Structure. Several distinct elements are held together in this account of the Ascension. A question from the disciples opens the scene in v. 6. Then, in vv. 7-8 Jesus speaks to the disciples (for the last time as an earthly communication), correcting them, making them a promise, and then, giving them a mandate. Verse 9 narrates the Ascension of Jesus in graphic terms. In vv. 10-11 the disciples are given an interpretation of the meaning of the Ascension by "two men in white robes" who have appeared suddenly. After hearing these messengers, the disciples (including the eleven, women—especially Mary the mother of Jesus—and members of Jesus' family) return to Jerusalem where they are united in prayer, awaiting the promised Spirit. Their return sets up the following account of the miracle at Pentecost.

These verses open and close by focusing on the disciples, and in between we hear the words of Jesus and the words of the two men—between which the Ascension takes place. Thus the material is shaped so as to frame and accentuate the Ascension:

A disciples
B Jesus to disciples
C Jesus' Ascension
B́ men to disciples
Á disciples

Significance. This entire passage is woven together carefully for profound theological reasons. A strong negative lesson comes through in several related items: The disciples' question, "Lord, is this the time when you will restore the kingdom to Israel?" comes on the heels of Jesus' promise of the Holy Spirit (Acts 1:5). And Jesus' answer denies the validity of their (seemingly reasonable) curiosity about when God's work will be consummated. The Spirit that Jesus promises does not come to empower the disciples to privilege but to service as witnesses of Jesus Christ. Christians are not called to futile speculation about the timing of God's work, rather they are called to do the work to which Jesus Christ commissions them.

The manner in which Acts explicitly narrates the physical removal of Jesus is unique in the New Testament, and there is a clear purpose in the story. The telling of this event firmly associates the anticipated eschatological restoration of the kingdom to Israel with the parousia. The two men put it bluntly, "This Jesus . . . will come in the same way as you saw him go into heaven." Moreover, in this story Jesus departs on "a cloud." This singular cloud matches the description of the coming of the Son of Man on "a cloud" with power and great glory in Luke 21:27—not on "clouds" as in Mark 13:36 or Matthew 24:30. The risen Jesus has been exalted (through the Ascension) to a position of universal power and authority.

All of this assures the disciples of God's ultimate triumph in and through the lordship of the crucified, raised, and ascended Jesus Christ. He is exalted into heaven and is the source of the promised Spirit. This means that Jesus does not merely belong to the past. He has not ascended into absence. He belongs to the present and has authority over the future. He is present, though not in his former earthly body, through the Holy Spirit and the work of his disciples, whom he charged to become his faithful witnesses. Indeed, the witness to which disciples are commissioned is the declaration of God's work through the telling of Jesus' story—including the truth of Christ's lordship.

There are many other striking elements in this story that are worth consideration. Notice that Jesus not only anticipates that the disciples will be faithful in proclaiming the message, but he tells them to work to the very "ends of the earth." Christ calls us to global missions as well as to daily Christian living. Notice the presence of the two "angels" at the Ascension. The disciples are not left to ponder the significance of the Ascension. Christianity is not a guessing game. God's purposes are plainly enough revealed that we need not ponder ourselves into inactivity. Finally, notice the rich mixture of the earliest band of disciples—followers, friends, and family—united anew in prayer. Faith unites us in mutual devotion to our Lord.

The Response: *Psalm 68:1-10, 32-35*

God, the Lord, Is King

Setting. Interpreters often refer to this psalm as the most striking, difficult, and obscure text in the psalter. Whatever the form of this text, it is unique among the psalms. Many scholars conclude that the text is in fact an incoherent assemblage of first lines from an older collection of hymns, a set of directions for worship. It is helpful, however, to note that vv. 24-25 state the occasion in which this text functioned—a glorious worship procession in which the kingship of the Lord was declared and celebrated. With such a setting in mind, even if the bulk of the psalm is a list of song titles, one can imagine the militantly festive character of the worship for which this text was intended. The presence in the psalm of both common ancient Near Eastern images for divinity (for example, ''him who rides upon the clouds'') and the mention of ''the girls'' as participants in the procession (v. 25) may indicate this text is at least, in part, quite old.

Structure. Interpreters suggest various schemes for the organization of this material. A fairly common suggestion is that vv. 1-3 are a prelude that declares the fierce power of God and calls the worshipers to celebrate God's power in joy. Verses 4-14 assemble a series of images related to God's providential activity and his accomplishments in the Exodus. Verses 15-16 are a haughty celebration of God's choice of Zion. The remainder of the psalm comprises sections that treat God's kingship and his relation to Israel and the nations.

The sentences of this psalm appear random or disconnected, at times. In vv. 4-10 commentators often suggest that v. 4, vv. 5-6, and vv. 7-10 are separate units of thought. If the response is incorporated into the liturgy, one might choose a short unit of thought rather than the entire psalm. Verses 32-35 are quite doxological.

Significance. The kingship of God and the Lord's assumption of kingship in Zion is the theme of this psalm, no matter what view of the structure one adopts. The God of the psalm is a mighty but compassionate king named ''the Lord.'' The divine king of Israel is presented as one with the power to overwhelm enemies and as one in whom the righteous can rejoice. Thus the standards of God's reign are those of righteousness, and those criteria separate God's enemies and God's people. Remarkably it is not clear that God's enemies are merely nasty humans; indeed, many of the images suggest that the text is celebrating God's power that defeats the larger forces of wicked chaos, which would include some creatures but not be restricted to them.

Over and over these lines call the worshipers to exuberant jubilation. The images from the Exodus and the entry to the promised land come into play as God's leading of the people through the wilderness is cast as if it were a festal procession. This celebration is not meant merely to recall a past event; rather as the worshipers remember God's past saving actions and celebrate them, they experience the events once again in the present. Israelite worship was more than memorial ceremony; it was the present claiming of the real power of God, which had acted in the past to achieve salvation.

New Testament Texts

The two New Testament lessons provide a fitting conclusion to the Easter Season. Each text describes what it means for disciples to be in relationship with the risen Lord and how our relationship with God must redefine our lives in this world. I Peter returns one last time to the theme of suffering, while John 17:1-11 explores what it means for disciples to embody the glory of the risen Lord.

The Epistle: *I Peter 4:12-14; 5:6-11*

Post-Easter Vigilance

Setting. The rhetoric of our texts shifts for this Sunday, which has prompted many scholars to suggest that the Baptismal Sermon (1:3–4:11) ends and a more direct address begins with I Peter 4:12, which then continues through 5:11. This demarcation may be accurate if we observe that the unit begins with the address "Beloved." In any case, there is a shift in mood, and the topic of suffering becomes a more immediate challenge. If I Peter has underscored anything for us during this Easter season, it is that the life of Christian faith in the Kingdom of God is not a party. There is a real conflict in this world between good and evil, which is being played out in the realm of human action. The concluding lesson from I Peter brings this reality home. The shift in mood conveys the immediate presence of real suffering, and the message of the author in this situation is that no form of evil should surprise the Christian.

Structure. The lesson for this Sunday requires that we forge together two texts that are not immediately joined, even though they are related thematically. The overall theme that could be used to relate the two texts may be summarized as, "Don't be surprised, be faithful!" The two texts can be outlined in the following three-part structure:

I. Don't Be Surprised (4:12-14)
   A. The Christian's Response to Unexpected Suffering (vv. 12-13)
      1. Do not be surprised (v. 12)
      2. Rejoice to share in Christ (v. 13)
   B. The Power of God (v. 14)
      (The power of the name)
II. Be Faithful (5:6-10)
   A. The Christian's Response to Unexpected Suffering (vv. 6-9)
      1. Christian and God (vv. 6-7)
         (Be humble/Don't be anxious)
      2. Christian and evil (vv. 8-9)
         (Be sober and watchful/Resist in faith)
   B. The Power of God (v. 10)
      1. To restore
      2. To establish
      3. To strengthen
III. A Doxology (5:11)

Significance. Notice how the first two parts of the outline (I and II) are in a parallel structure, which consists of an exhortation for Christians to respond appropriately to suffering and of a theological rationale for action.

First Peter 4:12-13 sketches in a few brush strokes a situation of surprise and thus of vulnerability. The audience of the letter has experienced persecution that has gone beyond the boundaries of their expectations, and it raises the question, What is to be made of such suffering? The author responds in v. 12 that it is not something to be surprised at because it is not at all a strange thing. This response still leaves us with the question, Why this suffering? Verse 13 does not really answer the question, rather it focuses the audience's attention beyond the experience of suffering to the past suffering of Christ and the future hope of glory.

The parallel text in I Peter 5:6-10 does address the problem of suffering more directly, while it also provides detailed advice on how Christians must resist the evil that accompanies suffering. This section separates into two parts: the Christian's relationship to God (vv. 6-7) and the Christian's relationship to evil (vv. 8-9). The first part picks up the focus on God that was introduced in 4:13, with two commands that are interrelated. During times of unexpected suffering, Christians must be humble to God, which means that they must give their anxieties to God. Christians behave this way, according to the author, because God is not indifferent to suffering and, in fact, is actively opposing the evil that causes it. The second part states why there is any suffering. The active presence of God in our world ensures conflict between good and evil. Christians, therefore, should never be surprised at suffering, because in Christ we have actively joined the conflict between good and evil. Participation in this conflict requires sober watchfulness and resistance by means of faith.

Second, we are offered a theological rationale for resisting evil. Victory is not the reason for participating in the present conflict. Rather joining the fight is the only way that we can be joined with Christ. First Peter is not a celebration of suffering. It is a celebration of salvation in Christ. First Peter 4:14 and 5:10 make this point clear by underscoring how Christian action is rooted in the glory of God both in the present and future time. This reality (that God is active in our world and will bring this conflict to an end one day) allows the text to shift to doxology even in the midst of unexpected suffering.

There is energy in this text that must be conveyed in preaching it. Suffering here is not simply a defensive posture against evil that must be endured by Christians. Rather, it is the result of Christ's aggressive action in the world through his Passion, which we, the Church, willingly choose to join.

The Gospel: *John 17:1-11*

A Prayer for Disciples

Setting. John 17:1-11 is part of the intercessory prayer of Jesus, which is also called his high priestly prayer. This prayer concludes the last discourse of Jesus in the Gospel of John (chapters 14–17), from which our last two gospel lessons were also taken. After this final prayer for his disciples, the author of John will turn his attention to narrating the Passion of Jesus for the remainder of the Gospel (chapters 18–21).

Structure. There is significant debate on how to outline John 17. The lectionary text is only a portion of the intercessory prayer, which continues through v. 26. Even without the problems of structure that arise from studying the entire chapter, it is still difficult to determine the movement of vv. 1-11. The following outline is one way in which the unit might be structured:

     I. Jesus and Glory (vv. 1-5)
    II. Jesus and Disciples (vv. 6-8)
   III. Disciples and the World (vv. 9-11)

Significance. The three-part division underscores the intimate interrelationship between Jesus and his disciples, between the glory that Jesus received through his Passion and the mission of his disciples.

Verses 1-5 focus on the glory of Jesus. The motif of glory occurs five times in as many verses, and it has a two-part meaning in the Gospel of John: Glory is a (1) visible manifestation of majesty (2) through acts of power. Jesus requests in vv. 1-2 that the Father glorify him, so that he, in turn, may glorify the Father. In vv. 4-5 Jesus states that he has already glorified the Father on earth through the work that he has accomplished and that in view of this he now wishes to be glorified in the very presence of the Father. In following the movement of the text, it becomes clear that the glory of Jesus is already loose in this world (v. 4), and that his further request for glory concerns the vindication or exaltation of the work that Jesus has already accomplished. This further glorification of Jesus in the presence of God ties his work back to the Father.

Verses 6-8 shift the focus from Jesus and glory to Jesus and his disciples. This shift is possible because Jesus' glorification with the Father provides the link between the disciples and the Father. This knowledge is the content of the disciple's faith, which results in a life of obedience.

Verses 9-11 draw out the implications of the knowledge that the disciples receive from Jesus. Two things stand out. First, since knowledge inevitably leads to a life of obedience, it will be inevitable that the disciples will be in conflict with the world. Jesus makes this separation between world and disciples clear in v. 9, by singling out his disciples as being the object of his prayer. Second, through their knowledge, which must lead to action, the disciples will become an extension of the glory of Jesus that has already been let loose in this world. The result of this knowledge is that the Christian community will be one in the glory of Jesus much like Jesus and the Father are one.

The high priestly prayer of Jesus contains ideas that are similar to the text of I Peter. It conveys the same idea that the Church's conflict and suffering in this world are because the power of Jesus is let loose. Thus both texts evince a certain energy in suffering, not to idealize it for its own sake but because suffering bonds the Church to the aggressive mission of Jesus. I Peter ties the Church to the prior Passion of Jesus, while John bonds the Church to the future glory of Jesus.

Easter 7: The Celebration

Preachers frequently seem a little embarrassed and apologetic about preaching on the Ascension. Forty days earlier they stood in the pulpit and declared that "Christ is risen!" Now they have scruples about just how high! The problem may have to do with the Lukan chronology that separates (as John does not) a unified mystery into component parts: Resurrection, Ascension, and empowerment. And of course the problem has to do with our enlightened, scientific worldview, so we feel under some compulsion to explain the Ascension in a way that we avoid when explaining the impact of the Resurrection. It helps when we "spiritualize" the Resurrection, because then we are not required to ditch the body from the pulpit, although the credal affirmation about belief "in the resurrection of the body" continues to make things awkward for us. God's seeming preoccupation with the material will not easily let us escape the implications of these events.

Karl Barth suggests that what changes about Christ in the mystery of the Ascension is simply the place, the vantage point, from which he operates. He moves from a human place to a divine place without ceasing to be human, just as he did not cease to be divine in this human place. To concentrate on the direction of movement in a spatial sense is to miss the point. This movement places our humanity in the presence of divinity; it is a glorification not only of Christ, but of all human nature. Political systems argue for human dignity from many angles. Christianity demands human dignity not because of any rights we may believe ourselves to have, but because our worth is derived from the humanity that is a part of the Godhead. The exaltation of the incarnate Christ, says Barth, "refutes all attempts at setting up another government, another 'place,' from where orders and promises would reach us. It is the ultimate refutation of all dictatorships" (*The Faith of the Church,* p. 98).

St. Leo, in a sermon on the Ascension, points out that Christ's departure to another place now makes possible for everyone his ongoing sacramental presence: "Our Redeemer's visible presence has passed into the sacraments. Our faith is nobler and stronger because sight has been replaced by a doctrine whose authority is accepted by believing hearts, enlightened from on high. This faith was increased by the Lord's ascension and strengthened by the gift of the

Spirit.'' So even in Christ's physical absence, there is still a material, sacramental presence to prevent us from too easily ''spiritualizing'' or cerebralizing the faith.

For congregations celebrating the Eucharist today, Dix's hymn, ''Alleluia! Sing to Jesus'' will reflect many of these themes.

Pentecost

Old Testament Texts

Pentecost Sunday provides a fitting conclusion to the Easter Season because it shifts our focus from Christ to the Holy Spirit, from the event of salvation to the breaking in of a new creation. The linking of Easter and Pentecost is a strong affirmation of how salvation and creation are inextricably related. The Old Testament texts provide important commentary on the central relationship of salvation and creation. Numbers 11:24-30 explores how the people of God structure community, while Psalm 104:1*a*, 24-34, 35*b* is a celebration of this fact.

The Lesson: *Numbers 11:24-30*

Authority in the Christian Community

Setting. Numbers 11:24-30 is a story about prophetic authority. As is frequently the case when the power of God's spirit becomes the point of focus in scripture, there is ambiguity and tension concerning the recognition of the power of the Spirit with regard to (1) who can have it and (2) how we know that the power is genuine. The larger context of vv. 4-35 accentuates the ambiguity of this story.

Structure. Numbers 11:4-35 is a murmuring story, in which Israel (or perhaps better, "a rabble" within the group) complains about not having meat to eat in the wilderness. Never mind that they are presently being kept alive by the miraculous gift of manna. This is not the first murmuring story, so the reader is not overly surprised by the thematic development of murmuring. What is new to the story is that Moses becomes angry in vv. 10-15 to the point that he contemplates death as a better alternative to leading Israel.

The complaint of Moses in vv. 10-15 concerning the burden of leadership provides the link to the subtheme of prophetic leadership in vv. 16-30, which divides between vv. 16-23 and 24-30 (the text for this Sunday). Verses 16-23 provide an important context for the lectionary reading. These verses divide between 16-20 and 21-23. Verses 16-20 constitute God's response to Moses' complaint. He is instructed to gather seventy elders and bring them to the Tent of Meeting where they will be given a portion of Moses' spirit. Moses is not assured even by this distribution of power and questions in vv. 21-23 whether there is enough food anywhere to feed this group of 600,000. God's response to Moses provides the immediate context to the lectionary text: "Is the Lord's power limited?" (v. 23). The question is left hanging.

The lectionary text separates into three parts: vv. 24-25, 26-27, and 28-30. Verses 24-25 describe the empowerment of the seventy elders. They receive a portion of Moses' spirit and prophecy momentarily to demonstrate their power before they (presumably) take up their leadership roles. Verses 26-27 is unexpected. It is as though the spirit of God splashes over the preestablished boundaries of the seventy elders and lands on two others, who begin to prophesy independently. Verses 28-30 provide two responses to the unexpected effects of God's spirit. Joshua is against it and Moses is in support of it.

Significance. Numbers 11:24-30 is about power and authority within the community of the people of God. The emphasis on prophetic authority with its unpredictable charismatic aspect provides an excellent avenue for preaching on Pentecost. The story provides two central insights concerning how we view authority within the Christian community. These insights are represented negatively in Joshua and positively in Moses through their exchange at the close of the text. Furthermore, through their responses each character provides an answer to the divine question ("Is the Lord's power limited?") that was placed to Moses in v. 23 but never really answered.

Joshua: Joshua's actions imply a yes answer to the question

concerning limitation on divine power, and as such he meant to provide a foil to Moses. Note how the writer has gone to great lengths to spell out Joshua's important credentials. He is the assistant to Moses and one of the seventy elders. He is part of the power structure that has been established with its clear and controllable boundaries. His reactions to the unexpected prophesying of Eldad and Medad are negative. "Stop them!" he commands Moses. Is the Lord's power limited according to Joshua? Clearly yes, and thus the unexpected prophesying cannot be tolerated.

Moses: Moses is the ideal in this story. He is presented as affirming the orderly distribution of power through the seventy elders, and he is open to the surprises of the spirit as evidenced in Eldad and Medad. Thus he responds to Joshua with a question of his own, "Are you jealous for my sake?" Then he concludes the story by idealizing the unpredictable aspect of prophetic authority by wishing that all of Israel might have the power of Eldad and Medad.

Numbers 11:24-30 is an excellent story for probing the charismatic power of God's spirit on Pentecost, because it affirms both the power of structure (seventy elders) and the surprises of God (Eldad and Medad). Too often the charismatic power of God is set over against institutional structures of the Church. This dichotomy is not an accident, since an essential aspect of the Spirit is its unpredictability. Such a quality means that established structures can be undermined. Or, as the writer of John tells us, the Spirit blows where it will, thus it cannot be contained within set boundaries. The manner in which Moses is idealized in Numbers 11:24-30 is helpful on Pentecost Sunday, because it encourages us to expand our understanding of the spirit as power set loose both in established structures and in other unexpected places.

The Response: *Psalm 104:24-34, 35*b

Celebrating God's Creative Power

Setting. Psalm 104 is a hymn celebrating the creative power of God. It shows a connection to Genesis 1 in vv. 6 and 25 as well as to creation motifs from other cultures in the ancient Near East. Verses

19-24 have a marked resemblance to the Egyptian hymn of Akhenaton (Amenophis IV 1200 B.C.E.?), especially with the encyclopedic listing of aspects of creation. In addition references to primeval waters, vv. 6 and 26 also suggest the influence of flood mythology from Syro-Canaanite primeval flood mythology.

Structure. Scholars debate the structure of Psalm 104 and the reader is encouraged to consult some commentaries for discussion of the full range of problems. The lectionary text includes the opening half verse of the psalm, which is a statement of praise and most probably three concluding sections: vv. 24-26, 27-30, and 31-35. The text can be outlined in the following manner:

I. Introductory Praise (v. 1*a*)
II. Praise of God as Creator of the Sea (vv. 27-30)
III. Praise of God as Sustainer of the Earth (vv. 27-30)
IV. Concluding Praise (vv. 31-35)
    A. Call for Continued Theophany (vv. 31-32)
    B. Promise of Praise (vv. 33-34)
    C. Concluding Invective (v. 35)

Significance. Psalm 104 is a celebration of God's power as creator. The three concluding sections of the psalm shift the focus somewhat by describing different aspects of God's creative power. Verses 24-27 describe the power of God over sea creatures and even the mythological sea monster Leviathan. Verses 28-30 move from sea to land to underscore how God's creative power is also evident in the continuation of life cycles on earth. Finally, vv. 31-35 provide summary in three ways: first the poet requests the continuing care of God for creation; second, there is a vow to praise God the Creator; and finally, there is a concluding invective. The function of this invective is to pull the psalmist's meditation on creation back into the moral sphere. Contemplation of God's work in creation has moral implications for humans.

New Testament Texts

How many times were the disciples anointed with the Holy Spirit? Was Jesus present among them, ascended into heaven, or both? The lectionary makes a bold move in bringing these texts together, for they are not easily harmonized or reconciled. The Roman Catholic Church has struggled with the relationship of these passages at least since the Second Council of Constantinople in 553 c.e., recognizing two real gifts of the Spirit, one private and related to the forgiveness of sins, the other public and related to the directing of the Church's mission of evangelism. Unless one insists upon driving a skeptical wedge between these texts, Protestants may well learn from Roman Catholic tradition at this point.

The Text: *Acts 2:1-21*

Knowing God's Presence and Having the Courage to Name It

Setting. The setting of this text was treated at length in the material for the Second Sunday of Easter, and readers should turn again to that material. Here we comment on the setting of the entire Pentecost story in the overall structure of Acts. In Acts 1 we moved from Easter up to Pentecost, seeing the risen Lord present among the disciples, instructing them, and promising the coming of the Holy Spirit. Acts 2 narrates the fulfillment of Jesus' promise, and it shows us quite dramatically what the disciples do as a result of being anointed with the Spirit—they are transformed from being mere eyewitnesses to being genuine ministers of the word. The remainder of Acts, beginning in Acts 3, tells how certain faithful disciples continue the Christ-ordained and Spirit-empowered mission.

Structure. General remarks about the structure of this passage are in the material for the Second Sunday of Easter. There are three distinct sections in this lesson: 2:1-13, 14-16, 17-21. Verses 1-13 have three subsections that provide a narrative introduction to Peter's speech in vv. 14-40. First, we learn of the time and place (v. 1) and, second, vv. 2-4 tell dramatically of the coming of the Holy Spirit upon the disciples. Third, vv. 5-13 introduce and describe the assembly of "devout Jews from every nation" and tell of the mixed reaction of the crowd to the disciples. Verses 14-16 fix the speech in relation to

Jerusalem, Pentecost, the cosmopolitan crowd, and then we receive statements about the divine anointing of believers, the ensuing miracle(s), and the misunderstanding of the masses. Verses 17-21 correlate the events of Pentecost with scriptural texts that provide a biblical interpretation of the incidents that are recounted in the Acts of the Apostles.

Significance. Peter claims that prophecy clarifies the Pentecost happenings; he identifies divine activity and the presence of the Holy Spirit with the effects on the believers. This allows him to name the time as "the Last Days." In turn, this naming of the time indicates the crucial nature of the Pentecost as a moment of cosmic crisis and divine judgment. The outcome of the eschatological outbreaking of the Spirit at Pentecost is the driving of humanity to call on the name of the Lord in order to be saved.

Notice the boldness of Peter's speech at Pentecost. He made several points clear in this speech, and at least two prominent points are inherent in this week's lesson: (1) Only those in a positive relationship to Jesus Christ—as the one in whom God's plan was/is fulfilled—are in a position to understand properly the present work of God. The masses could not comprehend the effects of the Holy Spirit on the believers, because they had no knowledge of the promise of the risen Jesus that the Spirit would come upon the disciples. The superior knowledge of the disciples is not a source of privilege, but a call to service in behalf of Christ to the masses. Christianity is not gnosticism. Whatever we know by the grace of God is given to us to direct us to ministry. (2) Christians have a peculiar and particular perspective on time: it is the Last Days—a penultimate time of fulfillment, judgment, and salvation. An important dimension of the ministry to which we are called is the naming of the times. Time from the Christian point of view is not a spiral, or a circle, or even a mere line. Time belongs to God, who changed the time in the life, death, Resurrection, and Ascension of Jesus Christ and the subsequent outpouring of the Holy Spirit. The time of God's promise has been brought to fulfillment. In the current moment, described in the lesson as "the last days," we live under the plain claim of God. The declaration of Peter means that God's work which humanity hoped had, in fact, already broken into history so that things were no longer the same.

Furthermore, as there is a difference between the time of God's present and the time of the past, brought about by the activity of God, there will be a difference between the present and God's future. We do not simply wait on God, for God in Christ and the Spirit has come in a real, significant way; but God's coming is not fully present and will not be until "the last day." In the present, we are called to name God's presence, to change our lives through the power of the Spirit so that they are given in obedience to God's active will, and to look forward confidently and courageously to God's future even amidst less than perfect circumstances.

The Gospel: *John 20:19-23*

Jesus Changes, Empowers, and Redirects Lives

Setting. The author of the Fourth Gospel carefully crafts the post-Resurrection appearances of Jesus. After the discovery of the empty tomb by Mary Magdalene (20:1), she informs the disciples that the body is missing (v. 2). Peter and the beloved disciple run to the tomb, and after entering they (or the beloved disciple) believed, but Mary was not present (vv. 3-10). In turn, Jesus appears to Mary and she believes (vv. 11-18). At evening, Jesus appears to the disciples, who are overjoyed (vv. 19-23); but Thomas was not present (vv. 24-25). In turn, Jesus appears to the disciples and Thomas, and Thomas believes (vv. 26-29). Verses 30-31 of John were likely the original ending of the Gospel.

Structure. This lesson is a subtle combination of story and pronouncement. Verses 19-20 narrate the appearance of Jesus to the disciples by telling of the location, the fear of the disciples, the miraculous manner of his appearance, his issuing of "peace" to them, his showing the signs of his crucifixion, and the disciples' joy. Verses 21-23 form a second portion of the story, marked off by Jesus repeating the words, "Peace be with you." In turn, Jesus commissions the disciples, breathes the Holy Spirit on them, and empowers them for the ministry of the forgiveness of sins.

Significance. This brief text is heavy-laden with significant theological themes that are best held together both for deeper comprehension and to avoid misunderstanding. John begins by noting the fear of the disciples. We should start thinking about this passage by recognizing that emotion. Yet, this is not just any fear; this is fear related to religious persecution. Analogies should be to historical examples of persecution for religious reasons. In the midst of that fear, the Lord appears. His real presence brings peace and joy to the disciples. The peace comes as the risen Jesus bears and pronounces the peace of God into the lives of the disciples. This peace is brought or created. It is not conjured up from some faded part of the disciples' lives. Jesus does not say, "Cheer up." Moreover, the joy is also a result of the presence of Christ, but more specifically it is the result of the disciples' identifying the risen and present Lord with the crucified Jesus. Seeing the nail scars moves the disciples from fear to joy.

Having brought and pronounced peace, the risen Christ commissions the disciples. There is no careful definition of the "sending" of which Jesus speaks, but we should notice that the disciples are sent by Christ and like Christ. As God sent Jesus, so Jesus sends the disciples. God's purposes in sending Jesus are now extended as Jesus sends the disciples. In other words, the concerns of Jesus' own ministry, as it is known through the Gospel according to John, are to be the concerns of the work of the disciples. This line of thought continues as Jesus breathes the Holy Spirit upon the disciples. He had worked in the power of the Spirit, and now the same Spirit is given to the disciples after Jesus commissions them. And the words of the risen Lord continue to provide clarity about the sending of the disciples when, in v. 23, we hear the enigmatic pronouncement about the forgiveness of sins. What exactly is Jesus empowering the disciples to do? Are they now to play God? No. In Greek, the precise construction of these lines tells that it is ultimately God who does the forgiving, through the power of the Holy Spirit, which has come upon the disciples to empower and direct them. The passive forms of the verbs, "are forgiven" and "are retained," assume the hand of God. The authority operative in this ministry of forgiveness is a continuation of the ministry of Jesus through the work of the Holy Spirit. Thus the forgiving of sins by the Holy Spirit working through the disciples is the bestowing of the very salvation provided by Jesus himself through his life, death, Resurrection, and gift of the Spirit.

Pentecost: The Celebration

The move from white paraments to red and the use of an Old Testament lesson again can give this day the feel of a new season rather than that of a triumphal conclusion to the Great Fifty Days. This is not altogether inappropriate, however, and one can easily understand how for centuries in the Church's practice the Day of Pentecost was thought of as the beginning of a new season. It is understandable because the theme of Pentecost is the new creation, the new thing that God is doing in the world. Yet this new creation is inextricably tied to the Easter event, as today's Gospel makes clear. The work of the Holy Spirit that we are celebrating is the continuation of the ministry of Christ. Without that connection we are apt to lose our Trinitarian balance and overemphasize a vague worship of the Holy Spirit. This connection with the work of Christ is also a corrective against statements like, "Pentecost is the coming of the Spirit into the world," as though the Holy Spirit had not been here from the beginning. Pentecost is the celebration of a specific work of the Spirit, which is the empowerment of the Church for Christ's service in the world.

It is for this reason that the Holy Spirit is called upon by the Church when we intend to perform some serious work. At ordinations we sing the "Veni, Creator Spiritus". The Great Thanksgiving at the Eucharist, the Thanksgiving over the Water at baptism, and the ordination prayers all have sections known as the epiclesis, a portion of the prayer where God is asked to grant the work of the Holy Spirit in effecting our requests.

If the Eucharist is celebrated today, the following epiclesis might be sung by the congregation immediately following the minister's said epiclesis in the Great Thanksgiving. The text is by Charles Wesley and should be sung to an appropriately vigorous tune such as Azmon.

Come, Holy Ghost, thine influence shed,
And real make the sign;
Thy life infuse into the bread,
Thy power into the wine.

Effectual let the tokens prove
And made, by heavenly art,
Fit channels to convey thy love
To every faithful heart.

Today's Gospel can also provide an opportunity for the worship committee to discuss the meaning of passing the peace and to see it not as an exercise in group dynamics or community building, but as a liturgical participation in the peace that comes from the risen Christ and not out of our own good humor. This means that it needs to be located with care within the service, so that it is seen to be the work of Christ in our midst. Usually this would be after the words of forgiveness following the prayer of confession or after the dismissal and blessing at the conclusion of the service.

Scripture Index

Old Testament

Apocrypha

New Testament

A Comparison of Major Lectionaries

YEAR A: ASH WEDNESDAY THROUGH THE DAY OF PENTECOST

	Old Testament	Psalm	Epistle	Gospel
ASH WEDNESDAY				
RCL	Joel 2:1-2, 12-17	51:1-17	II Cor. 5:20b-6:10	Matt. 6:1-6, 16-21
RoCath	Joel 2:12-18	51:3-6, 12-14, 17	II Cor. 5:20-6:2	Matt. 6:1-6, 16-18
Episcopal	Joel 2:1-2, 12-17	103		
Lutheran	Joel 2:12-19	51:1-13	II Cor. 5:20b-6:2	
THE FIRST SUNDAY IN LENT				
RCL	Gen. 2:15-17, 3:1-7	32	Rom. 5:12-19	Matt. 4:1-11
RoCath	Gen. 2:7-9; 3:1-7	51:3-6, 12-14, 17		
Episcopal	Gen. 2:4b-9, 15-17, 25–3:7	51		
Lutheran	Gen. 2:7-9, 15-17; 3:1-7	130		

	Old Testament	Psalm	Epistle	Gospel
THE SECOND SUNDAY IN LENT				
RCL	Gen. 12:1-4*a*	121	Rom. 4:1-5, 13-17	John 3:1-17
RoCath	Gen. 12:1-4	33:4-5, 18-20, 22,	II Tim. 1:8-10	Matt. 17:1-9
Episcopal	Gen. 12:1-8	33:12-22		
Lutheran	Gen. 12:1-8	105:4-11	Rom. 4:1-5, 13-17	John 4:5-26 (27-30, 39-42)
THE THIRD SUNDAY IN LENT				
RCL	Exod. 17:1-7	95	Rom. 5:1-11	John 4:5-42
RoCath		95:1-2, 6-9	Rom. 5:1-2, 5-8	
Episcopal	Exod. 17:1-7			
Lutheran	Isa. 42:14-21	142	Eph. 5:8-14	John 9:1-41
THE FOURTH SUNDAY IN LENT				
RCL	I Sam. 16:1-13	23	Eph. 5:8-14	John 9:1-41
RoCath	I Sam. 16:1, 6-7, 10-13			
Episcopal			Eph. 5:(1-7)8-14	John 9:1-13 (14-27) 28-38
Lutheran	Hos. 5:15-6:2	43	Rom. 8:1-10	Matt. 20:17-28

	Old Testament	Psalm	Epistle	Gospel
		THE FIFTH SUNDAY IN LENT		
RCL	Ezek. 37:1-14	130	Rom. 8:6-11	John 11:1-45
RoCath	Ezek. 37:12-14	130	Rom. 8:8-11	John 11:1-45
Episcopal		130	Rom. 6:16-23	John 11:(1-17) 18-44
Lutheran		116:1-8	Rom. 8:11-19	John 11:1-53 or
				John 11:47-53
		THE SIXTH SUNDAY IN LENT (PASSION/PALM SUNDAY)		
RCL	Isa. 50:4-9a	31:9-16	Phil. 2:5-11	Matt. 26:14–27:66 or 27:11-54
RoCath	Isa. 50:4-7	22:8-9, 17-20, 23-24	Phil. 2:6-11	
Episcopal	Isa. 45:21-25 or 52:13–53:12	22:1-21	Eph. 1:3-6, 15-19a	Matt. (26:36-75) 27:1-54 (55-66)
Lutheran		31:1-5, 9-16		Matt. 26:1–27:66

THE EASTER VIGIL (OR EASTER DAY)

		Old Testament	Psalm	Epistle	Gospel
RCL	[1]	Gen. 1:1–2:4a	136:1-9, 23-26 or Ps. 33		
	[2]	Gen. 7:1-5, 11-18; 8:6-18; 9:8-13	46		
	[3]	Gen. 22:1-18	16		
	[4]	Exod. 14:10-31; 15:20-21	Exod. 15:1b-6, 11-13, 17-18		
	[5]	Isa. 55:1-11	12:2-6		
	[6]	Bar. 3:9-15, 32–4:4	19		
	[7]	Ezek. 36:24-28	42–43		
	[8]	Ezek. 37:1-14	143		
	[9]	Zeph. 3:14-20	98 or 114	Rom. 6:3-11	Matt. 28:1-10

	Old Testament	Psalm	Epistle	Gospel
RoCath [1]	Gen. 1:1–2:2	33 or 104		
[2]	Gen. 22:1-18	16:5, 8-11		
[3]	Exod. 14:15–15:1, 15:1-6, 17-18			
[4]	Isa. 54:5-14	30:2, 4-6, 11-13		
[5]				
[6]		19:8-11		
[7]	Ezek. 36:16-28	42:3, 5; 43:3-4 118:1-2, 16-17, 22-23	Rom. 6:3-11	
				Matt. 28:1-10
Episcopal [1]		33:1-11 or 36:5-10		
[2]				
[3]		33:12-22 or 16		
[4]	Exod. 14:10–15:1			
[5]	Isa. 4:2-6	122		
[6]	Isa. 55:1-11	Ps. 42:1-7 or Isa. 12:2-6		
[7]				
[8]		30 or 143		
[9]	Zeph. 3:12-20	114	Rom. 6:3-11	Matt. 28:1-10

	Old Testament	Psalm	Epistle	Gospel
Lutheran [1]	Gen. 1:1–2:2			
[2]				
[3]				
[4]	Exod. 14:10–15:1a			
[5]				
[6]	Baruch 3:9-37			
[7]	Ezek. 37:1-14			
[8]	Isa. 4:2-6			
[9]	Exod. 12:1-14			
[10]	Jonah 3:1-10			
[11]	Deut. 31:19-30			
[12]	Dan. 3:1-29	Song of the Three Young Men	Col. 3:1-4	Matt. 28:1-10

THE SECOND SUNDAY OF EASTER

	First Reading	Psalm	Epistle	Gospel
RCL	Acts 2:14a, 22-32	16	I Pet. 1:3-9	John 20:19-31
RoCath	Acts 2:42-47	118:2-4, 13-15, 22-24		
Episcopal		111 or 118:19-24		
Lutheran		105:1-7		

THE THIRD SUNDAY OF EASTER

	First Reading	Psalm	Epistle	Gospel
RCL	Acts 2:14a, 36-41	116:1-4, 12-19	I Pet. 1:17-23	Luke 24:13-35
RoCath	Acts 2:14a, 22-28	16:1-2, 5, 7-11	I Pet. 1:17-21	
Episcopal	Acts 2:14a, 36-47	116		
Lutheran	Acts 2:14a, 36-47	16	I Pet. 1:17-21	

THE FOURTH SUNDAY OF EASTER

	First Reading	Psalm	Epistle	Gospel
RCL	Acts 2:42-47	23	I Pet. 2:19-25	John 10:1-10
RoCath	Acts 2:14a, 36-41		I Pet. 2:20-25	
Episcopal	Acts 6:1-9; 7:2a, 51-60			
Lutheran	Acts 6:1-9; 7:2a, 51-60			

	New Testament	Psalm	Epistle	Gospel
	THE FIFTH SUNDAY OF EASTER			
RCL	Acts 7:55-60	31:1-5, 15-16	I Pet. 2:2-10	John 14:1-14
RoCath	Acts 7:1-7	33:1-2, 4-5, 18-19	I Pet. 2:4-9	John 14:1-12
Episcopal	Acts 17:1-15	66:1-11	I Pet. 2:1-10	
Lutheran	Acts 17:1-15	33:1-11	I Pet. 2:4-10	John 14:1-12
	THE SIXTH SUNDAY OF EASTER			
RCL	Acts 17:22-31	66:8-20	I Pet. 3:13-22	John 14:15-21
RoCath	Acts 8:5-8, 14-17	66:1-7, 16, 20	I Pet. 3:15-18	
Episcopal		148	I Pet. 3:8-18	John 15:1-8
Lutheran		66:1-6, 14-18	I Pet. 3:15-22	

	Old Testament	Psalm	Epistle	Gospel
THE SEVENTH SUNDAY OF EASTER				
RCL	Acts 1:6-14	68:1-10, 32-35	I Pet. 4:12-14; 5:6-11	John 17:1-11
RoCath	Acts 1:12-14	27:1, 4, 7-8	I Pet. 4:13-16	
Episcopal	Acts 1:(1-7)8-14	68:1-20 or 47	I Pet. 4:12-19	
Lutheran	Acts 1:(1-7) 8-14	47	I Pet. 4:12-17; 5:6-11	
THE DAY OF PENTECOST				
RCL	Num. 11:24-30 or Acts 2:1-21	104:24-34, 35b	I Cor. 12:3-7, 12-13	John 20:19-23
RoCath		104:1, 24, 29-31, 34	I Cor. 12:3-7, 12-13	
Episcopal	Acts 2:1-11	104:25-37 or 33:12-15, 18-22	I Cor.12:4-13	John 14:8-17
Lutheran	Joel 2:28-29	104:25-34	I Pet. 3:15-22	

A Liturgical Calendar

Ash Wednesday Through the Day of Pentecost 1992–2001

	1992–93 A	1993–94 B	1994–95 C	1995–96 A	1996–97 B
Ash Wed.	Feb. 24	Feb. 16	Mar. 1	Feb. 21	Feb. 12
Lent 1	Feb. 28	Feb. 20	Mar. 5	Feb. 25	Feb. 16
Lent 2	Mar. 7	Feb. 27	Mar. 12	Mar. 3	Feb. 23
Lent 3	Mar. 14	Mar. 6	Mar. 19	Mar. 10	Mar. 2
Lent 4	Mar. 21	Mar. 13	Mar. 26	Mar. 17	Mar. 9
Lent 5	Mar. 28	Mar. 20	Apr. 2	Mar. 24	Mar. 16
Passion Sun.	Apr. 4	Mar. 27	Apr. 9	Mar. 31	Mar. 23
Holy Thur.	Apr. 8	Mar. 31	Apr. 13	Apr. 4	Mar. 27
Good Fri.	Apr. 9	Apr. 1	Apr. 14	Apr. 5	Mar. 28
Easter Day	Apr. 11	Apr. 3	Apr. 16	Apr. 7	Mar. 30
Easter 2	Apr. 18	Apr. 10	Apr. 23	Apr. 14	Apr. 6
Easter 3	Apr. 25	Apr. 17	Apr. 30	Apr. 21	Apr. 6
Easter 4	May 2	Apr. 24	May 7	Apr. 28	Apr. 20
Easter 5	May 9	May 1	May 14	May 5	Apr. 27
Easter 6	May 16	May 8	May 21	May 12	May 4
Ascension Day	May 20	May 12	May 25	May 16	May 8
Easter 7	May 23	May 15	May 28	May 19	May 11
Pentecost	May 30	May 22	June 4	May 26	May 18

	1997–98 C	1998–99 A	1999–2000 B	2000–01 C
Ash Wed.	Feb. 25	Feb. 17	Mar. 8	Feb. 28
Lent 1	Mar. 1	Feb. 21	Mar. 12	Mar. 4
Lent 2	Mar. 8	Feb. 28	Mar. 19	Mar. 11
Lent 3	Mar. 15	Mar. 7	Mar. 26	Mar. 18
Lent 4	Mar. 22	Mar. 14	Apr. 2	Mar. 25
Lent 5	Mar. 29	Mar. 21	Apr. 9	Apr. 1
Passion Sun.	Apr. 5	Mar. 28	Apr. 16	Apr. 8
Holy Thur.	Apr. 9	Apr. 1	Apr. 20	Apr. 12
Good Fri.	Apr. 10	Apr. 2	Apr. 21	Apr. 13
Easter Day	Apr. 12	Apr. 4	Apr. 23	Apr. 15
Easter 2	Apr. 19	Apr. 11	Apr. 30	Apr. 22
Easter 3	Apr. 26	Apr. 18	May 7	Apr. 29
Easter 4	May 3	Apr. 25	May 14	May 6
Easter 5	May 10	May 2	May 21	May 13
Easter 6	May 17	May 9	May 28	May 20
Ascension Day	May 21	May 13	June 1	May 24
Easter 7	May 24	May 16	June 4	May 27
Pentecost	May 31	May 23	June 11	June 3